MILLENNIAL MOVEMENTS

T0335357

MILLENNIAL MOVEMENTS

Positive Social Change in Urban Costa Rica

KAREN STOCKER

Teaching Culture: Ethnographies for the Classroom

UNIVERSITY OF TORONTO PRESS

Toronto Buffalo London

© University of Toronto Press 2020
Toronto Buffalo London
utorontopress.com
Printed in the U.S.A.

ISBN 978-1-4875-8868-7 (cloth)   ISBN 978-1-4875-8869-4 (EPUB)
ISBN 978-1-4875-8867-0 (paper)   ISBN 978-1-4875-8870-0 (PDF)

Library and Archives Canada Cataloguing in Publication

Title: Millennial movements: Positive social change in
urban Costa Rica / Karen Stocker.
Names: Stocker, Karen, author.
Series: Teaching culture.
Description: Series statement: Teaching culture:
ethnographies for the classroom | Includes
bibliographical references and index.
Identifiers: Canadiana (print) 20200228560 | Canadiana (ebook) 20200231995 |
ISBN 9781487588687 (hardcover) | ISBN 9781487588670 (softcover) |
ISBN 9781487588694 (EPUB) | ISBN 9781487588700 (PDF)
Subjects: LCSH: Social action – Costa Rica – History – 21st century. |
LCSH: Community activists – Costa Rica – History – 21st century. |
LCSH: Costa Rica – Social conditions – 21st century. |
LCSH: Community leadership – Costa Rica –
History – 21st century. | LCSH: Youth – Political activity –
Costa Rica – History – 21st century.
Classification: LCC HN133.5.S76 2020 | DDC 361.7084/2097286 – dc23

We welcome comments and suggestions regarding any aspect of our publications – please feel free to contact us at news@utorontopress.com or visit us at utorontopress.com.

University of Toronto Press acknowledges the financial assistance to its publishing program of the Canada Council for the Arts and the Ontario Arts Council, an agency of the Government of Ontario.

Canada Council   Conseil des Arts
for the Arts   du Canada

ONTARIO ARTS COUNCIL
CONSEIL DES ARTS DE L'ONTARIO
an Ontario government agency
un organisme du gouvernement de l'Ontario

Funded by the   Financé par le
Government   gouvernement
of Canada   du Canada

Canadä

Contents

Illustrations

Acknowledgments

I wish to thank family and friends, both in Costa Rica and in the United States, who lent support throughout the research and writing process. In particular, thanks to friends in Costa Rica – Camila Vargas and Irene Pérez – for serving as a sounding board for these ideas as they unfolded. I also thank those who helped connect me to people, opportunities, and information, among them César R. Barrantes, Mario Molina, Mush, Joshua Álvarez, and the Grupo de Jóvenes Artistas de Matambú. California State University, Fullerton, offered sabbatical leave that made this research possible. I appreciate my supportive colleagues there, especially Barbra Erickson and those members of the Research and Critical Educators (RACE) group – in particular, Lucía Alcalá, Sarah Grant, Aitana Guía, and Satoko Kakihara – who offered feedback early on. Likewise, I extend my appreciation to colleagues and friends who offered insights during a fruitful writing retreat: Deborah Boehm, Julia Meredith-Hess, Mariela Nuñez-Janes, and Mariann Skahan. Thank you to the students of Anthropology 504 in Fall 2017 for robust discussions about ethnographic writing that helped shape initial versions of this work, to two graduate students – David Angulo and Marco Moreno – who read early drafts, and to artistic collaborators from Cog•nate Collective, Amy Sanchez Arteaga and Misael Diaz, who influenced my thinking. Thank you also to the anonymous reviewers, editors, and staff at University of Toronto Press, especially Anne Brackenbury and Carli Hansen. All of these individuals offered invaluable suggestions. The remaining errors are wholly mine.

Above all, I wish to thank the inspiring leaders, organizers, activists, and artists featured in this book. I dedicate this book to you, with gratitude.

1

Introduction

Along Fourth Avenue, a pedestrian boulevard cut in half by a newish, blue bike lane, the city bustled with people going about their business in San José, Costa Rica. Graffiti from the Ni Una Menos (Not One Less) protest against femicide from the 2018 International Women's Day march dotted the architectural landscape. Amid messages written by survivors and their allies to aggressors, like, "If sexism makes you uncomfortable, you are sexist" and "Not One Less," appeared an unusual combination of sentiments. On the wall of the historic girls' high school someone had scrawled the phrase, "Against patriarchal and capitalist violence," followed by a spray-painted description of this protest as "our happy rebellion" (*nuestra alegre rebeldía*). The declaration of happiness mingled with such a serious topic caught my eye. This mixture of protest and positivity was something I had researched for six months in 2016 while examining emerging social movements in San José, started by people in their twenties. But the International Women's Day march itself offered a contrast. Most of the social movements I studied did not take the form of protests carried out by masses of people, fueled by the justifiable discontent or anger often necessary to disrupt the status quo, with which I am more familiar. Instead, I would characterize these movements as solution-oriented while rooted in a positive outlook. They demonstrated a willingness of leaders to collaborate with anyone – whether other activist groups, government agencies, or corporations – committed to working towards a shared goal. They displayed a concern for environmental sustainability. They shared inclusive and non-hierarchical leadership styles. And they revealed a running theme of equitable appropriation of public space. Several of the movements were at once grassroots and globally infused. In some cases, their leaders traveled or earned university degrees abroad, then worked with their home community to identify needs and see how foreign programs might be adapted to meet them. The social movements I studied throughout 2016 applied international ideas to needs closer to home or sought to ameliorate local concerns circumscribed by global forces.

What I expected to be an investigation of distinct organizations, or *colectivos* as their young leaders called them, turned out to be part of a network of mutually supportive groups geared towards bringing about social change. Some were smaller-scale initiatives that individuals took on that, coexisting with other programs, lent strength to larger community actions. Some were social enterprises or private businesses that supported the goals of broader movements or that had an activist agenda. Others, networked via social media and in real life with other collectives and concerned with shared causes, were movements in the making. These individuals' and groups' initiatives served various social movements, including those endeavoring to bring about environmental sustainability and independence from fossil fuels; physical safety and freedom from sexual assault; economic security for farmers; food insecurity for urbanites; environmentally, culturally, and economically sustainable business practices; mitigation of homelessness; revitalization without gentrification; public art and graffiti as cultural resources; building inclusive communities; and LGBTQ+* rights.

While these groups addressed topics that fit my preconceived notions of which themes social movements would take on, they challenged my other expectations. I went to San José, Costa Rica, in

---

* A sign made by the Centro Cultural de España en Costa Rica, and posted around San José, urged people to "complete your language," by adding IA to this label. However, the identities more readily addressed by collectives in San José were those denoted by the letters, "LGBTQ+." In cases where only some of these identities were addressed, I will use different configurations of letters to indicate this. This inconsistency is purposeful, in the name of accuracy.

2016 to study several movements that had emerged in that city in recent years, whether independently or following the lead of movements begun elsewhere in the world. Eduardo Silva (2015, 29) offers a working definition of social movements as "loose networks of activists and supporters with low levels of organization in which power is horizontal that favors protesting over engaging the political establishment." He goes on (Silva 2015, 30) to consider that social movements are, then, "agents of reform." The collectives I studied would call into question some parts of this definition and uphold others.

They clearly sought and effected change, and they used horizontal organization strategies in leadership, utilizing inclusivity as a strategy. They recognized young people and individuals with varied backgrounds as being experts on their own lives, as having insights and energy to contribute to society, and as being capable of leadership. The groups I studied were highly organized and did not always resort to protest, though the Ni Una Menos (Not One Less) march described at the outset of this chapter reveals that such forms of protest also occurred in Costa Rica. Likewise, I witnessed strikes staged by teachers and by nationalized taxi drivers undercut by the privatized, transnational ride-sharing industry. The taxi drivers protested through absence: a roadway roundabout usually surrounded by the constant snaking of red taxis and characterized by the blaring of horns went eerily silent and empty. In contrast, the teachers' union, while on strike, overtook the area in front of the Legislative Assembly one day through their crowded, overwhelming presence. An animal rights group and the Diversity Movement, not yet called Pride, held march-like events. But the marches, too, struck a positive tone. Amid signs shouting NO MISTREATMENT OF ANIMALS, poodles in tutus and dogs otherwise clad for a festive occasion participated in a political event that was more a pet parade than an angry demonstration. This deliberately upbeat flavor is one characteristic of the social movements in Costa Rica that marked these initiatives as distinct from the no longer novel, so-called New Social Movements of the 1980s, which drew from anger as a source of strength to clamor for change (see also Choudry 2015, 9, 15; Munson 2008, 67).

Coming from the United States accustomed me to taking an activist stance in keeping with the ways these sentiments are commonly expressed in my country, such as strikes, marches, and public protests, enacted as a reaction to unjust policy or practice. Given that experience, I considered that anger is not only an understandable point of departure for current and long-standing struggles but, more importantly, that it serves as a necessary driving force to keep these movements going in the long term. Ann Berlak (Berlak and Moyenda 2001, 110) distinguishes between moral anger and defensive anger, noting that the former stems from "socially induced suffering" as opposed to defensive anger, which "is a response to being held (or feeling one is being held) accountable for the injustice that provoked the moral anger in the first place." There is no doubt that moral anger can serve a critical purpose in organizing. Social movements that seek to redress police brutality exerted disproportionately against people and communities of color or organizations that take on the various forms of violence engendered by extreme social class disparities have good reason for anchoring their efforts in moral anger. Highlighting yet a different affective point of departure, philosopher Slavoj Žižek (2018) asks readers to consider the merits of hopelessness for understanding those concerns around which movements coalesce, and Andrea Muehlebach (2012) addresses the role of loneliness as a mobilizing force for social engagement. Movements stemming from a passion for a cause offer another emotional source of action.

Yet movements rooted in other emotions, sometimes in concert with outrage, have been present throughout Latin American history. Sparked by concern – in addition to outrage – about social issues, historically, they won public favor by strategically emphasizing maternal love or obligation (see Escobar and Alvarez 1992). Movements that draw strength from affect – be it anger, hopelessness, or happiness – may be variously positioned to take on different sorts of issues. What's more, they may mix. Activists from North America may appreciate the deliberate use of humor in the form of signs and placards at marches amid those more strident in tone, each emotive root offering its own form of serious critique. Likewise, North American protest participants may revel in moments of joy even within actions rooted in anger. These need not be mutually exclusive endeavors. They may combine within the same event or be used sequentially: activists engaged in prolonged, necessary-but-wearying forms of protest, due to their in-depth work against systematic oppression, may use strategies rooted in happiness as momentary respite to remain engaged in social change while renewing energy and avoiding burnout (see Lopez Bunyasi and Smith 2019, 212).

Rather than using emotions such as joy as ephemeral oases within movements more characteristically marked by anger, San José's more recent movements reverse this ratio, demanding new policies and practices geared towards social change while maintaining a positive tenor as a constant. This is not surprising, perhaps, in this officially pacifist nation-state so frequently ranked first in the annual Happy Planet Index. One millennial leader cocked her head to the side as I asked her about the influence of the happiness characteristic of Costa Rica on her model of seeking social change. *"Puede ser,"* Andrea* assented – it could be – but it had not previously occurred to her (see chapter 3). Like the majority of these groups' leaders, Andrea started an initiative geared towards social change when she was in her twenties. The age of their respective leaders was another defining characteristic of these collectives. These were millennial movements; by example, their leaders contested presiding stereotypes about the age group of people born in the 1980s and subsequent decades, between the ages of eighteen to thirty-five at the time of this study (see Cairns 2017, 6, 7). Youth activism is not a new phenomenon (see Kirshner 2015); the movements highlighted here follow this trend. They showcase young people who identified a social need, strategized ways to address it, and then got to work, maintaining an optimistic, proactive approach throughout the process.

These discourses, as well as deeper concerns, surround the millennials in Costa Rica. They experience the stereotypes of a generation-based label as well as the benefits and detriments of globalization. They are the first generation to grow up in an era marked by climate crisis, and it will be primarily up to their generation and those that come after them to contend with these effects and to find solutions to them. Many of the leaders highlighted in this book share similarities with North American millennials in the way that internet-based technologies have existed throughout their lifetime. However, Costa Rican millennials may have

---

* Some of the first names of leaders used in this book are pseudonyms and some are not, depending on the preference of each interviewee.

gained access to those technologies more recently than their North American counterparts. Still, at the current moment, they make skillful use of internet-based social networks in order to connect to global movements, local participants, and support from both realms, as well as from the intersections thereof. As is the case for young people in North America, sometimes globalization's effects are positive and sometimes not, depending on an individual's or their community's social and economic position among them. Yet these leaders opted to highlight positive effects to lessen the impact of negative ones, perhaps as an influence of their existence within a country that banks on its image of happiness.

But while happiness as a marketed feature of national identity is one possible root of this pattern among social movements in Costa Rica, there are also other likely sources. San José is located in the middle of a nation-state committed to pacifism, having officially abolished the military in 1949, and it strives to make education and health care available to all of its citizens. The government maintains price protections on basic food items considered common to all households, and government programs offer hot meals to pre-school age children and nursing mothers in the most vulnerable communities, thus addressing concerns about food insecurity. These characteristics have contributed to Costa Rica's relative stability. Its oft-cited slogan of having more teachers than soldiers remains a point of pride for citizens, although it does not reflect a flawless educational system. After all, rural-urban divides, socioeconomic disparities, and varied forms of discrimination still show their effects (see Stocker 2005). Likewise, a health care system involving small clinics in rural villages, which are connected to regional hospitals and centralized medical facilities dedicated to specialized care, though imperfect, does assure that social class is not the determining factor of one's chances of meeting health care needs. Neither does stigma rooted in health status: all HIV-positive individuals have a legal right to antiretroviral drugs. And the entire country enjoys potable water, a relative rarity in Latin America. Access to recreational enjoyment of ocean water is likewise guaranteed to all citizens, who have a right to use public land, including beaches that have become home to multinational hotel chains. In the political sphere, Costa Ricans enjoy equal representation by gender, as every democratically elected level of government, from city councils upward, has a legal obligation to attend to gender equity. Laborers have a legally recognized right to strike and unionize. In the realm of environmental well-being, the government actively promotes sustainability as a national goal. Recently, Costa Rica extended its goal of carbon neutrality by the year 2021 to having zero emissions by 2050.

These examples show that some social goods and services currently fought for elsewhere are already built into law in Costa Rica. These entry points to relative security, some of which are the results of past activism and protests, may constitute one reason why contemporary social movements in Costa Rica can maintain a focus on creating positive change through dialogue, small-scale action, and an insistence upon optimism as central organizing strategies. These social guarantees, perhaps, have led to a lesser level of urgency than experienced elsewhere in the world. In turn, this relatively reduced precarity for vulnerable communities may allow for an emotion other than fury to propel social movements.

Yet being proactive or positive in focus did not necessarily result in displays of cheerfulness. For many of the emerging social movements, it simply meant carrying out steady work towards change for the better, or active engagement towards finding long-term solutions to salient problems. These movements are marked by praxis: philosophical outlook matched with action, in the name of generating transformation. These groups engage with hope not as a vapid wish but as something to be produced, deliberately, to be enacted as part of a collective responsibility. While a positive stance is something expressed by the leaders, they are not naïve about the pace of change and they harbor no illusions that optimism alone, without purposeful, corresponding work, will bring about tangible solutions. Neither are the leaders dismissive of the very real constraints upon Costa Rica's efforts towards inclusiveness and equity.

In spite of governmental efforts, Costa Rica is not a utopia. Costa Rica's placement within a global economy, and its international treaties and connections, such as the Central American Free Trade Agreement, threaten its economic autonomy and exert pressure to privatize some of the public programs that currently secure its relatively high degree of well-being. This threat has perhaps prompted the simultaneous, independent genesis of various collectives that urge the support of local producers, be they farmers, artists, or entrepreneurs. Likewise, they promote local products and local language. Indeed, this emphasis on bolstering the local was a commonly stated goal of various leaders. These millennial movements seek to address inequities not only felt as a result of Costa Rica's position in a global system but also evident within Costa Rica's and San José's internal stratifications.

San José, the capital city of Costa Rica, is a microcosm of the various subcultures that compose Costa Rican society. It is economically, racially, ethnically, and linguistically diverse, much like any other cosmopolitan capital city. The Greater Metropolitan Area, as San José and neighboring urban realms are known, comprises a mere 4 per cent of the nation-state's geographic expanse, yet houses over half of Costa Rica's total population, totaling more than two million people (Rodríguez Vargas 2016, 158). As is common for urban metropolises, this city is a place filled with the majority of the nation's people, but on a fraction of the land. As Arlene Dávila (2004, 15) reminds us, "cities are central to understanding the cultural politics of multiculturalism, the formation of new forms of participatory politics, and the potential realization of a just multicultural society." This is certainly the case for San José.

The coexistence of diverse groups, however, does not mean the city is free of inequities. Positions of power in San José, by and large, are still held by people who are of European descent and middle or upper class, thus indicating the persistence of privilege rooted in social class, race, and ethnicity, and its corresponding unearned, greater access to representation. This exclusion is felt most deeply by immigrant populations from nearby Nicaragua, Panama, Colombia, and Venezuela, and, increasingly, the continent of Africa; working-class Costa Ricans, including those dependent on the informal economy as roving vendors; LGBTQ+ community members cast out of their families of birth or otherwise excluded for nonconformity to cisgender or heteronormative expectations; and other groups disenfranchised from structures of power. Some of the leaders of collectives described here may subvert this trend or at least use their privilege to work towards greater inclusivity.

The middle-class or advantaged status enjoyed by leaders of some of the social movements described in this book gave them ready entrée to government, and, therefore, the ability to engender change. Several of these leaders are privileged, White, university educated, multilingual Costa Ricans with access to bank loans and funds to lease buildings or donate supplies or time. Indeed, various leaders spoke about privilege directly and without prompting. Yet many of those who traveled and studied outside of Costa Rica for a prolonged time in Europe or North America also experienced a shift from being privileged in their home country to being recategorized on the margins of society elsewhere, both for coming from Latin America and from Costa Rica, a small Central American country. The insight stemming from this should not be underestimated. This perhaps made them aware of their relative favored status (social class-based, racial, gendered, or otherwise, depending on the leader in question) at home. Their transnational experiences may have prompted insights that let them foresee some obstacles to social change and take care to establish coalitions across the divides present in San José, in their efforts to promote the appropriation of public space for "the people." But who made up "the people" was a question implicit in the various sites where people gathered for the initiatives described in this book.

While people coexisted in public space, it was not equally inviting to all. The gathering spaces used by social movements, enterprises, or initiatives described in this book are emblematic of these simultaneous spaces for the coming together of diverse groups and also for the inequities among them. Along Avenida Segunda, the place of the Pride march with a celebratory feel, marchers shared space with those people who looked on in disapproval. The Steinvorth building, named for its wealthy developer, in the heart of the city, sits amid the hubbub, quiet and clean inside. Those revitalizing it want it to be used by the people. But which people? A VIP event there blanketed with a red carpet fit for celebrities, and even the coffee shop where I would write field notes, might be off-putting to some of "the people" of the city, the people who defined it before its revitalization.

The Temple of Music in Parque Morazán has a name that might be jarring for many people in this officially Roman Catholic nation-state. But indeed, its name seems fitting. Jugglers, musicians, and dancers fill it in the evenings, appropriating the public park for the people, as intended, reverent of its public nature. Central Park, dotted with families, taxi stands, shoeshine workers, and police, exists around a monument described as being donated by "a Nicaraguan industrialist" (Low 1999, 122). It is actually from Anastasio Somoza, the decades-past dictator whose oppressive regime led to civil war, the many effects of which spurred emigration to Costa Rica. The monument he donated is right there in Central Park, the one where xenophobic Costa Rican citizens might judge Nicaraguan immigrants. National Park, in contrast, features a centerpiece monument to Central American nations, together, ousting William Walker and his US imperialist designs. Parque España, La Plaza de la Democracia, Avenida Central, and other gathering spaces equally proved to draw people from all walks of life, but not necessarily with equal ownership of the city. The collectives described here are trying to change that.

Whom "the people" encompassed varied from one leader to the next. In some cases, "the people" included refugees, the underemployed, the homeless, and immigrant communities, documented or not. For most, it meant Costa Ricans of all social classes and ethnic and racial backgrounds. For others, it implied a more exclusive realm. In the case of one interviewee, "the people" seemed to be implicitly synonymous with people who spoke fluent English, people with cable television who were current on *Game of Thrones*, with enough extra money to pay an entrance fee to see the final episode of one season projected on a big screen, and people who would refrain from discussing soccer. This is not the group I think of when I consider *"la gente"* of Costa Rica, after decades of interaction at informal gatherings, chatting over coffee at kitchen tables, and spending time with families of varied social classes and ethnicities, across the country. Whatever the definition, these efforts to make San José a space for "the people" will have varying degrees of success. Likewise, they will differ in their relative disruption of the status quo.

Recognition of persistent inequities and the forms they take may make some readers uncomfortable. Tourists to Costa Rica sometimes receive my research with displeasure, not wanting to imagine anything negative about a place that felt like paradise to them. I understand: I, too, love it. But believing it to be perfect sells it short as something other than a real place, where life is lived, not just escaped. It is in the spaces of imperfection that we may create solutions. Readers who have visited Costa Rica as tourists may also recognize a disjuncture between that which they read here, of the city's problems, as well as its innovative solutions, and what they saw while on holiday. What I write about here is the part of Costa Rica that visitors may not see; it is a cityscape only minimally marketed to tourists.

Surfers on beaches; horseback-riding, swimsuit-clad White tourists on sand to match, by clear turquoise waters, at sunset; conical volcanoes, with ash rising dramatically; waterfalls, cascading upon women in bikinis: these are a few of the images sold to tourists. The multicolored wheel of an oxcart, beside its driver, in trademark white, brimmed canvas hat: these are visual representations of living culture equally advertised to tourists. On occasion, the oxcart drivers from rural communities meet up to travel slowly, in caravan, to a work party, in a tradition that is beginning to gain visibility within national tourist circles. The rest of the year, they use their oxen without performing culture for others. And photos of beaches used to draw tourists leave out the Costa Rican families from the nearby countryside, wearing casual clothing, seated on chairs they brought, in the shade, away from the water's edge. They also will have brought with them all the food they will need during their beach outing, as paying tourist prices in businesses filled with foreigners may not be economically feasible.

One of the country's volcanoes, a feature of guidebooks and postcards, no longer erupts, but the images sold of it stay at once frozen in time and perpetually active: a paradox scripted for tourists. None of the advertisements present the daily domino game in a rural general store, or the retired/laid-off/injured/broken banana plantation workers who have retreated to cobbled-together houses on family land or uniform government grant houses, speckling the road that runs along small villages, far from the urban center. Equally out of view of the tourist gaze are the young leaders in San José, creating change in the city, the same city where most of the arriving tourists will land. In trying so hard to market *pura vida*, Costa Rica's signature phrase about a laid-back attitude, a value placed on well-being and purity of life, tourist images leave out the pureness – or at least the accuracy – of life as lived there.

Scenarios presented throughout this book may run contrary to readers' preconceived notions of Costa Rica as all tourism, all beaches, all rainforest, and allow them to see part of Costa Rica that the average tourist does not. In doing so, I want to invite readers into a portion of Costa Rican culture that is not the stuff of vacations but is the backbone of daily life for most of the nation's inhabitants. And it is this non-vacation view of Costa Rica that may resonate most with readers' own lives. Challenging stereotypes is one strength of ethnography, which lets readers see how themes in faraway places also apply to home. This book strives to do just that. The primary methods used in cultural anthropology aim to see cultural phenomena both from the outside in and the inside out. The view from a distance that this book offers readers in North America may allow them to then see their home environment in a new light.

Ethnographic methods are unique in that they require living within the research in a prolonged manner, to try on, for a time and to the extent possible, the culture under study. It comprises a set of strategies that rest upon thorough preparation, but also a commitment to flexibility. Ethnographic methods, in this way, involve an iterative process. Beginning long before departure, cultural anthropologists work to design a project that is ethically sound and approved as such by our host institution. This process involves thorough study of a topic ahead of time so as to develop interview questions thoughtful enough to draw out conversation yet open-ended enough to make room for possible responses the researcher has not yet considered. It also includes culturally specific considerations of obtaining participants' informed consent.

Having carried out ethnographic research in Costa Rica regularly since 1992 allowed me to refine my topic prior to beginning this particular study. While the research in this book represents, primarily, six months of intensive interviews and participant observation from 2016, twenty-four years of prior study informed it, as have follow-up visits since. My more than a quarter-century of experience in conducting ethnographic research in Costa Rica has offered me sufficient context and local knowledge to witness the emergence of social movements new to San José and understand the cultural and historical concerns that gave rise to them. Indeed, I have been observing and participating in Costa Rican society for as long as the leaders of these collectives have. Likewise, my long-term engagement with Costa Rican culture, and connections to people within it, facilitated my access to social networks both on the ground and online, so that I might interview leaders from various facets of society.

Once in the field site, the ethnographer needs to balance adherence to research design with adaptability, while figuring out how research-as-planned resonates with research-as-lived. An ethnographer simultaneously follows up on connections built in advance and cultivates new ones. In this project, I had met and held preliminary conversations with some young activists prior to designing the study. After arriving in Costa Rica in 2016, it was important to study the work they were taking on without getting in their way. To that end, I made an effort to work around leaders' schedules. In between scheduling and interviewing, I waited. But waiting, too, can yield productive time.

During that wait time, I followed the advice of my late mentor to see and be seen by walking the landscape. When Dr. Ilse Leitinger gave that advice, I was working in a tiny community of 121 people, which meant that walking would lead to being seen and talked about by everyone. This would help me become a normal sight in a small town and eventually facilitate my interviewing at least one person per household. In a city of over two million people, this would not work quite the same way. While walking would help me become familiar with a place, I had to figure out how to get a sense of salient patterns in thought among city-dwellers, without being able to interview one per household. In this study, walking the landscape allowed me to see changes that had happened since my previous visits, and to see the presiding sentiments written on walls.

Central concerns of the city became apparent as I read the graffiti around me, not only the fanciful murals and artful depictions signed with pride and ownership, but the kind scrawled by anonymous, amateur nighttime scribes making their voices heard in public. Messages reading, "No more assault" and "It's not a catcall, it's sexual harassment" spoke to everyday sexism in the city. By the Temple of Music, in one of San José's many green parks, on a long, curved bench, someone had written a cursive call to action, "*Pensando me gustas; haciendo te amo*": Thinking, I like you; doing, I love you. Written criticisms of the Central American Free Trade Agreement, Costa Rica's ratification of which was extremely contentious and divisive, and that threatens to undermine local endeavors in favor of multinational ones, divulged the economic backdrop of the groups I would study. Stenciled in white block letters against the gray concrete of the pedestrian boulevard on Central Avenue, the Habitantes de la Calle – Inhabitants of the Street – could catch the eyes of passers-by who might turn away from homeless individuals. A simple heart spray-painted in black next to the capital word TRANS offered a message of love and acceptance for a group that confronts hatred often. Green wording comparing the pineapple industry to the mining industry revealed an environmentalist agenda.

In more elaborate paintings, a mural by artist Negus Arte Vida featured a supine woman begging for spare change, asking, *"Una monedita?"* In primary colors, along a long wall showcasing murals, a work by Stephanie Chaves offers a mélange of bodies, trans individuals, police officers, and others, in an apparent allegation of corruption and police brutality (see figure 1). A wall full of fanciful faces urges, through dialogue box, that viewers, "Eat fruits and vegetables." Along the Wall of Fame, used by renowned graffiti artists in the university town, a small Black child cries a large, pendulous tear. Hein_Uno, the artist, reported onlookers telling him he should not depict the child as sad because childhood ought to be a happy time. Resolute in his artistic vision, Hein_Uno kept the tear and added a pixilated pinwheel design to disrupt such halcyon views of childhood. It should be happy, he agreed, but when it is not people need to see that, too. A piece by Gabriel Dumani, working alongside an international, Central American crew, offers a triptych – in poetry and in cartoonish, graphic imagery – of the realities of working in call centers for multinational corporations. And artist Chinox painted two purple orchids – the national flower – and a pregnant belly, in a place that lauds motherhood. The result was other than intended: criticism rang out from people who said two flowers could not have a baby, and from voices that reflected both homophobia and resentment towards IVF procedures rendered newly legal by mandate of the Inter-American Court of Human Rights. Some of these images may have been intended as political, and others became read as such in spite of artists' intentions. Either way, they spoke to the concerns of social movements emerging in San José.

Once I began more formal, semi-structured interviews with urban leaders, it became clear that some of these same spray-painted sentiments undergirded the movements I would research. I began interviews with people I already knew through prior research connections, and then took advantage of Costa Rica's small size and closely networked population. The first person I interviewed shared contacts with me openly and vouched for my trustworthiness as a

1 Mural by Stephanie Chaves

researcher to other leaders whom I interviewed subsequently. Paired ethnographic methods of interview and participant observation eventually allowed me to see how the anonymous graffiti, themes of signed murals, and various social movements intersected, offering a distinctly local understanding of culture while also bearing the mark of foreign influence. To research these connections and their effects, I conducted interviews with leaders and participants of nineteen different collectives and participated in more than eighty activities, including brainstorming sessions, meetings, tours, and mural painting, that would allow me to experience, first-hand, these organizations' strategies for leadership.

This combination of participant observation and interviews allowed for comparison between what people said and what people did. Living in the city where these leaders were taking action invited reflections on their contributions to city life and placemaking (see Basso 1996) outside of work hours. To further my understanding of the strategies I learned from young leaders, I enacted them myself in another of my long-standing field sites to see how these same tactics could be applied outside an urban realm to different sets of concerns (see chapter 8). Taken together, these methods led to the portrayals of social movements and their constitutive initiatives, enterprises, and actions presented here. These snapshots highlight particular themes and organizational strategies and serve as examples of ethnographic work and activism. Each chapter will focus on a particular social movement or collective. As case studies, they are specific to the place and time in which they existed or continue to exist and should not be generalized to all realms. However, I encourage readers to consider which elements of them might work well in their own communities.

This book focuses on social movements and the actions that comprise them in Costa Rica for a variety of reasons. From the perspective of the researcher, Costa Rica became the focal point of inquiry because it is where, over the course of decades, I have put in the time and effort necessary to earn trust and develop deep cultural understandings of the context in which these movements are taking place and the change they represent. It is the site where I have ample expertise to interpret culture. This adds to the credibility of this research. Long-term engagement in this realm also led to connections with interviewees and their respective networks. This depth of study is what sets ethnographic research apart from more superficial forms of interview-based inquiry. Yet a focus on Costa Rica is not only beneficial to this researcher.

North American readers who are activists already may benefit from examining these cases from another country by augmenting the range of activities they employ now. Urban Costa Rica offers enough similarity to other global cities more familiar to readers and overlaps sufficiently in terms of the degree to which current technologies infuse life, to offer additional strategies that may transfer well from a realm farther away to one closer to home. At the same time, the Costa Rican context may be different enough from North America to invite activists there to reflect on their home country and add to their spate of practices, by applying the tactics outlined in this book to local concerns. North American activists will learn how cultural anthropology and its signature methods are useful for activists, even if they are not anthropologists. Readers interested in becoming anthropologists will come to see how the methods of their discipline may be useful for becoming active in social movements. For those readers who are neither activists seeking additional methods to enact change, nor anthropologists intrigued by activism, there remains value in cross-cultural study. By examining a foreign one, one learns about their own culture, indirectly.

And yet, an underlying idea of this book is that society needs more individuals – whether or not they identify as activists – to get involved in helping to bring about lasting change within contexts that affect us all. This book rests on the understanding that those who already identify as activists will keep doing their part, and this book may offer additional strategies for carrying out that work. As a society, if we want more people to get involved, as will be necessary to ameliorate the climate crisis and other large-scale social issues that affect all of humanity, we need to expand existing avenues for involvement. There are three relatively easy ways to bring this about.

First, we know that people who may not identify as activists might join an effort because of their social connections; they attend a meeting or event because a friend is going, and once there, they learn about a cause (Munson 2008, 49, 52; Fisher, Svendsen, and Connolly 2015, 56, 58–9, 67–9; see also Engler and Engler 2016, 150). By making this known, this book may spur activists to keep inviting friends, or using social media to display their own involvement, or otherwise use their respective peer networks to generate more activism. If we create more ways to be an activist – whether or not people identify with that label – we then create more ways to get friends involved; we generate more platforms for individual activism; and we make it so that out of a wide array of forms of activism, people will be more likely to identify one that resonates with who they are and how they might be comfortable participating. Once there, they might be more likely to expand their manner of involvement, transcend their initial comfort zone, and get involved in additional causes, which is the second point.

We know that people already involved in activist causes are likely to join additional causes (Fisher et al. 2015, 83, 86, 117). This book will offer more ideas regarding how various movements might network to increase their participant base. It will offer examples of less wearying forms of activism to intersperse with North American activists' strategies, so as to stave off burnout and facilitate sustained involvement in a cause. Finally, activists are more likely to become active in civic engagement (Fisher et al. 2015, 83, 86, 117). From there, they can create systemic, institutionalized change. Even minimal participation in a feel-good endeavor, at the behest of a friend, may serve as a springboard to this development. The questions throughout this book guide students through considerations of how they might get started, however small in scope their initial project might be.

Different forms of activism may be well suited to varied concerns. Using multiple angles of affect, whether anger, fear, happiness, or some other emotion, to generate change may offer effective platforms from which to diversify one's efforts. The types of involvement presented in this book – some small-scale efforts and others that are more systemic – can work in tandem with larger-scale efforts to address the root causes of inequities. The efforts presented in this book represent real-world approaches undertaken by ordinary people seeking to make extraordinary change. The case studies featured here show steps that individuals or small groups of people can take to make a big difference.

Chapter 2 highlights a collective that promotes the appropriation of public space, and that offers an example of collaboration among groups to find a way to avoid gentrification in the city's revitalization efforts. Chapter 3 centers on a young leader whose organization endeavors to diminish reliance on fossil fuels and promote environmental sustainability in the urban sphere while striving towards gender equity. The chapter features strategies for uniting disparate stakeholders and demonstrates how small-scale projects can reach great success and even institutionalization. Chapter 4 focuses on how for-profit business can also play a role in developing environmentally, culturally, and economically sustainable practices that are also socially conscious. Chapter 5 introduces readers to a relatively simple project with a potentially large impact on hunger among marginal populations in the city, by channeling kindness towards those who need it most.

Chapter 6 shows how the methods of cultural anthropology mirror some of those used in activist endeavors. At the same time, it answers the question of what happens if these movements do not result in success as designed while showing that this is not tantamount to failure. Rather, leaders of small-scale organizations may use that experience as a beginning for bigger actions. Chapter 7, too, responds to critics' questions about the potential longevity of these movements by showcasing a leader who has demonstrated staying power. He shows what happened when the LGBTQ+ rights movement had to keep reinventing itself to adapt to changing circumstances. This chapter shows what happens when social movements started by young people grow up. Chapter 8, as well as the discussion questions at the end of each chapter, invites readers to consider how the strategies used in these case studies can be adapted to other sociocultural realms, including their own.

QUESTIONS FOR DISCUSSION AND ACTION

1. What forms of protest have you witnessed in your home country? How do they resonate with actions rooted in various types of affect introduced in this chapter? What sort of emotion lies at their core? What do you think are the relative merits of using anger vs. happiness, or other emotions, as a source of power? How might the underlying concern of a given movement affect the emotion best suited to address it?

2. The leaders featured in this book will offer us ways to counter presiding stereotypes about millennials. How do these relate

to stereotypes about Gen Z? How might you push back against generalizations about either generation?

3. This chapter presents various examples of graffiti, revealing the political sentiments of their artists. What messages does the graffiti around your city reveal?

SUGGESTIONS FOR FURTHER READING

On placemaking

Basso, Keith. 1996. *Wisdom Sits in Places: Landscape and Language among the Western Apache.* Albuquerque, NM: University of New Mexico Press.

On millennials and misplaced stereotypes

Cairns, James. 2017. *The Myth of the Age of Entitlement: Millennials, Austerity, and Hope.* Toronto: University of Toronto Press.

On the history of social movements in Latin America

Leitinger, Ilse A. 1997. *The Costa Rican Women's Movement: A Reader.* Pittsburgh: University of Pittsburgh Press.

Silva, G. Eduardo. 2015. "Social Movements, Protest, and Policy." *European Review of Latin American and Caribbean Studies* 100: 27–39.

ADDITIONAL RESOURCES

The Happy Planet Index: http://happyplanetindex.org/.
Marks, Nic. "The Happy Planet Index." TED Talks. 2015.
    https://www.youtube.com/watch?v=TnA_XxbyKEw&feature.

In this podcast, Christiana Figueres insists that a combination of "outrage and optimism" is key to reaching solutions to global crises:

https://podcasts.apple.com/gb/podcast/outrage-and-optimism/id1459416461.

2

Placemaking, Community Building, and Appropriation of Public Space

Roberto, the founder of ChepeCletas, was hurriedly unloading bicycles into the office already filled with bike racks, bike helmets, and, of course, the *cletas* – short for *bicicletas*: bicycles – when I arrived for the interview. He greeted me politely, following the manners common to a generation older than Roberto's millennial one. To explain his late start that morning, he let me know that a last-minute tour booking required him to rent additional bicycles from another bike-centered organization – one that in businesses with an opposite philosophical approach to that of ChepeCletas might be described as a rival company. I sunk into the couch placed in the middle of the office and took in the surroundings: message boards declaring I <3 Chepe (the affectionate nickname for San José), chalk drawings with the telltale signature of one of San José's most practiced street artists, and a large blackboard-turned-calendar noting other events around the city, ChepeCletas's own upcoming walking- and bike tours by day and by night, and the impending Pride march. A bright-colored chalk heart surrounded this last item. Even once Roberto was free, both the frenetic pace and his group's connection to other activist collectives would run as energizing themes throughout the interview.

Leaving the architectural beauty that was the ChepeCletas office in the historical heart of San José, diagonal from what was once a parking lot for oxcarts delivering sugar cane to the national liquor factory and parallel to the first city street to be graced with lamplight over a century ago, we walked briskly uphill, towards a coffee shop. We bustled past a side street looking onto the cartoonish, larger-than-life-size, primary-colored, painted image of a man stepping over the façade of a private business, past a mysterious metal door leading to the underground workings of the long-defunct liquor factory, alongside city walls emblazoned with paint, depicting animals astride bicycles, and a fading, once rainbow-colored, large cursive message reading, "Think for yourself." The conversation paralleled that fast clip, passing through topics such as public art and popular resistance, international influence over creative movements, and other young leaders to interview.

The pace of travel never lessened but did stop short once, in a way that revealed Roberto to be ever aware of the social environment of his surroundings. At the crest of a hill two blocks from the hospital, in an intersection with a flashing pedestrian symbol changing to red, situated in a microenvironment marked by car horns and impatience, two family members accompanying a woman in a wheelchair studied the abrupt shift from pedestrian crosswalk to steeper-than-usual curb with no ramp. Without missing a beat, and careful first to greet the women with the utmost courtesy, Roberto squatted to reach the front lower wheels of the chair and lift it up onto the curb, utter hurried well wishes for the ladies' day and goodbyes as if they were longtime family friends, before we continued on our way, turning quickly to the topic of inadequate walkability and access for disabled individuals of the city streets.

After a few blocks of uneven sidewalks, predictable only in their sudden dangers, we arrived at a coffee shop that participated in the Café Pendiente program (see chapter 5), a program that Roberto helped get off the ground, but for which he always defers credit to the young woman who founded it in Costa Rica. In a moment of rest demanded by a short wait in line, I ordered our coffees and two pay-it-forward coffees for strangers, while the owners/staff/baristas and Roberto greeted one another by name in apparent genuine mutual appreciation. We sat and the interview was then officially underway, though my brain already buzzed with insights from the arrival process alone.

In two hours, Roberto explained to me the beginnings of ChepeCletas, his pet project in placemaking (see Basso 1996). He and the two other people who co-led ChepeCletas began by doing night walking tours of historical sites around San José. In this country known for its focus on international tourism, ChepeCletas offers outings primarily to Costa Ricans, to explore their own city and reclaim it as such. This is important for two reasons. First, ChepeCletas began just as citizens prepared to vote in a referendum about Costa Rica's participation in the Central American Free Trade Agreement, a decision that culminated in increased foreign intervention in the national economy, sometimes to the detriment of local businesses. Second, and parallel in consequence, Costa Rica is a nation-state that serves as a primary ecotourism and adventure tourism destination for tourists from the world over. Costa Rica actively courts international tourism, and its citizens sometimes pay the price. They do so in terms of the elevated costs that come with an economy inherently linked to dollars and euros, and many Costa Ricans are quick to note that tourists get to see more of their country than they do. While ChepeCletas does work with tour companies catering to international tourists, their beginnings and their continued passion lie with the commitment to facilitate day trips for Costa Rican nationals around their own environment.

These excursions point out sites of historical interest hidden in broad daylight, masquerading as ordinary, and include visits to locally owned businesses bearing treats. But really, "History is just a *pretext* to draw people," Roberto explained, mostly in the familiar form of Costa Rican Spanish with an English word thrown in occasionally. Even in his language use, Roberto valued the local while showing global influence, a common trait of San José's emerging social movements. He explained that the goal behind ChepeCletas was "to appropriate space," filling it with people rather than police in order to bring about safety: "Full of people, [public space] is converted into safe space." His safety-in-numbers approach to national, urban sightseeing applies both to his organization's bike tours and walking tours. And his goal of appropriating space – making public space for the people in usage, not just in name – is working. He saw bike tours go from five to 500 participants in six years. Walking tours, likewise, have enjoyed increasing popularity. Roberto's unit of measure for success lies not only in numbers, however. Having worked against stereotypes of San José as dangerous and unwelcoming, he considers, "Every time one more person has a positive opinion of San José, that changes the perception of San José." That responds to another goal of ChepeCletas: in addition to appropriation of public space by the actual public, Roberto explained that the organization sought not only to "get to know new buildings," or come to know old buildings anew, as it were, "but to create a social space."

To that end, ChepeCletas has sponsored old-style dances of a sort common in his grandmother's generation, hosted in the iconic kiosk of a city park where such social functions used to be held. In this event, two concentric circles of party-goers shift to meet unfamiliar dance partners. Roberto described it in Spanglish as "*como un* speed dating." In its recent iterations led by ChepeCletas, young people danced with elders, and in a city with a decreasing reputation for friendly interaction and nighttime safety, strangers from distinct social circles not only shared space but danced together, at night, in the public park. Invoking another unusual unit of measure for success, Roberto noted that ChepeCletas has seen couples meet on their tours, first dates use their tours as a supportive platform for a nascent relationship, and even the first marriage of a couple who owes its beginning to a ChepeCletas meeting.

Taking advantage of his momentary break to sip coffee, I asked how he funded this endeavor. "It was crazy," he responded. Organizations approached ChepeCletas. "We've actually lacked initiative in that regard." Hotels and tourism agencies, as well as individuals, sought out ChepeCletas to lead tours. Private citizens and businesses approached them about leading events. Then the national tourism institute did the same. In spite of what Roberto's modesty suggests, however, the individuals behind ChepeCletas have also done their part. They have always reached out to local governments, which have, in turn, opened doors both figuratively and literally, to welcome tours of Costa Ricans to see locales dedicated to public service.

I pointed to this effort to build bridges with government as a salient difference between the social movements I saw in San José, Costa Rica, and those in my own country, where social movements commonly develop counter to or parallel to government entities, especially when governments are not doing their part to address an issue. Roberto confirmed that ChepeCletas has "a focus more in conjunction with, rather than in opposition to, the government." Unlike some purist North American social movements, also, but in keeping with the themes of the *colectivos* of San José, they pair with private businesses if a shared goal may be met that way. He noted that people's preconceived notions of bus drivers or their respective companies might not let them imagine the role of buses in promoting social movements led by progressive young people, but a major bus line has collaborated with them on those tours that take them out of a reasonable walking distance from the center of the city. In this manner, ChepeCletas promotes not only walking and biking but also use of public transportation among a clientele that may have grown dependent on the convenience of privately owned vehicles, thus abetting city congestion and the very problems faced by pedestrians and bikers. Related to this topic, ChepeCletas also does a fair amount of consciousness-raising in a manner that is more entertaining than sanctimonious.

In addition to working with municipal governments, the national-level governmental-run tourism institute, private businesses, and companies like a bus line that bridges private business with public interests, ChepeCletas also collaborates with other social movements. Working with Pausa Urbana, a group that shares ChepeCletas's interest in the appropriation of public space by the people, and also with established street artists, ChepeCletas sponsored an activity that beautified the otherwise imposing-looking metal curtains drawn down to secure the Central Market at night and on Sundays, when it is closed. Artists' efforts in this project came to function as a creative guard against gentrification, instead verifying the belonging of the market's long-standing figures at the same time that they invited a new, wealthier clientele to make use of the market.

Doña Ana stands outside the southwest corner of the Central Market, where she has done so at least six days per week since childhood. She pronounces her surname the old way, like her immigrant grandfather did, giving each double consonant its due. Most days are the same there, with roving vendors shouting advertisements for their wares, and then a scurrying and quick fitting in among shoppers when their network receives a warning that the municipal police is on the way. It used to be through coded whistles, but WhatsApp makes it easier these days. After they disperse – or stay in place, hidden as shoppers rather than vendors – it might be quiet for a time until the police move on and the vendors come back, shouting out, "The newest fidget spinners!" "Avocados!" "DVDs!" or whatever else they are selling that day. But in the times when it is quiet, the area surrounding the market is still bustling with passers-by on foot, going about their business, ever since Central Avenue was made into a pedestrian boulevard.

Most days, doña Ana stands there at the southwest corner announcing the lottery numbers she has available for sale or asking people what number they play, and they buy a couple of shares of any given number. Sometimes they dreamed about two drunken figures, swaying in tandem, walking side by side, and so they buy number 55. Some always play their anniversary. Some look at the leaves of a *lotería* plant to look for numbers coded in dots, to see what fortune the houseplant portends. And some, of course, go by their gut. Six days a week, doña Ana stands there, behind a small table, her hair done meticulously, in full makeup, and with her smart outfit covered with an apron, its pockets stuffed with cash. There, with each available portion of a lottery ticket number thumbtacked to the wooden top of her folding table, she works, daily, at the southwest corner of the Mercado Central. The mayor even designated her a *personaje de San José*, a noted figure; an icon, if you will.

It is not just out of habit that she stands there, on that corner. She has rights to it. She cannot own it, just like nobody can own a stall in the old marketplace – a rule that prevents gentrification within the market – but she has use rights. She has *derechos adquiridos* to sell lottery tickets on this site, like her father did before her, and like her grown son, who for now sells just a few meters away. But if there was any doubt that it was her corner before, some millennial artists made it plain for all to see (see figure 2).

While doña Ana and the roving vendors in her environ are exactly the type of local figures who get displaced when city officials decide to revitalize an area, instead making room for economic elites at the expense of the working class, the project enacted by ChepeCletas, Pausa Urbana, and several expert graffiti artists found a way to mirror, outside the market, the municipal rule that prevents gentrification within it.

Select artists, sponsored by the two *colectivos*, painted all of the doors and *cortinas metálicas*. The metal curtains drawn down over the marketplace's windows, and each of the eight entryways to the labyrinthine marketplace built in 1880, became adorned with portraits of people who have a place there by the market. There is Mr.

2 Portrait of lottery vendors painted by VIVO

Robinson, the man who was a beloved calypso singer before his mind went. For decades, he slept there, by the edge of the market sometimes. But nobody could ask him to leave; it was his place.* It bears his portrait still. And there are elders, painted onto the metal curtains, with their wheelchairs and walkers, and a sign spelling out *Dignity* in an elegant script. A disabled woman who frequents the market, walking on her hands, who sometimes asks for money and otherwise goes

---

* In 2019, after more than forty years on the street, Mr. Robinson died at the age of seventy-seven. *Que en paz descanse.*

about her business there, is painted on entrance number two; in fact, the municipal government demanded that her portrait be included when they approved the project. And there are others, each with their place, affirmed on the marketplace's metal shutters. This way, even when the market is closed at night and on Sundays, and even if they aren't present, one can see that they belong. With her own portrait, painted by VIVO, on the southwestern entrance of the Central Market, it looks like doña Ana even works on Sundays. And during the week, she stands there, double, the person in front of her portrait, like the Zs in her last name, each their own entity, but standing together.

This artistic emplacement of potentially vulnerable community members – immigrant, itinerant, or whose belonging might otherwise be questioned by those with the power to revitalize a district – was not by happenstance. Hein_Uno explained the careful research that went into his decision, alongside artist Jeancarlos Sequeira-Joker506, to paint Mr. Robinson's portrait, in keeping with his other efforts to get admirers of his street art to see sad realities too often overlooked in a culture that focuses deliberately on happiness. Like Hein_Uno, each artist chosen to work on the Central Market project decided who or what to paint there, effectively rooting onto the landscape those people who might be most prone to further marginalization in the application of some creative city models. This was less a case of artists appropriating space for their own work, as per their usual custom, than using their art to acknowledge space already appropriated and to be respected as such. This project was only one collaboration between ChepeCletas and Pausa Urbana. They also worked together to have a nighttime bike ride's ending point land at the celebration of local musical style *swing criollo* being danced in a public setting, to join efforts in encouraging friendly interaction among strangers in the city's public spaces. In this manner, they combined efforts in nighttime events that secured safety through numbers of participants, united in an effort to change attitudes about the city and activities that supported such a change.

Roberto rattled off the names of several other organizations with which ChepeCletas has cooperated, generously offering me contact information for their leaders, too, in an act demonstrating his promotion of collaboration and interaction once again. In response to my question about the seemingly simultaneous genesis of these grassroots organizations, and which social trends might have supported that, he said that the simultaneous independent invention of several of these organizations is a mystery to him, too. "Many of these groups started in 2009 or 2010. We ask ourselves what happened in 2010 [that served as a springboard for this], but we don't know. It's not that we coordinated it or anything." But since that spontaneous beginning of several emerging social movements, they have collaborated on many endeavors, for mutual support. He mentioned the Art City Tour, started by his friend, another young leader, to encourage museums and art venues to stay open late one night per month, offer free admission, and invite corporate sponsors to provide transportation among the various participating galleries and museums. This effort mirrors Chepe-Cletas's goals of getting people to make use of their city at night, and meet people with shared interests along the way. Roberto also spoke about Café Pendiente, the pay-it-forward coffee program (see chapter 5). Roberto concluded, "These alliances have been very valuable. It's like a community." Indeed, they share community building as a goal.

Through co-sponsorship and working towards a shared interest in positive social change, ChepeCletas has worked with other organizations and with the national Ministry of Transportation to bring about the existence of a bike lane in a city where just a few years prior this would have seemed an impossibility. Roberto stressed how important it is to "try to resolve issues through alliance." Through roundtables and meetings geared towards finding solutions in a positive manner, they have brought into being plans for urban mobility (see also chapter 3). They are tackling climate change and other matters related to environmental sustainability. They are working towards making a country greatly dependent on international tourism take into account not only beaches and zip lines but also a city with a deep history and a culture of its own to offer not just to tourists but to the people who reside there. But this has not always been an easy sell. Roberto explained that people who travel to Paris would be shocked if they disliked it. In contrast, tourists express surprise at liking San José. ChepeCletas is working to change that, and instead show that, like any other coveted urban destination, San José "is a city where we can find an identity." To this end, ChepeCletas is working to "create community."

Aware that I was taking time away from that admirable goal, I wrapped up the interview. We walked back, retracing the route we took to the coffee shop, still talking a mile a minute. From his office, I walked to my bus stop, and throughout the ride, scrawled field notes still spilling out of my brain, hopped up on caffeine and inspiration. In the shaky handwriting of notes taken on a moving bus, I wrote in my notebook, "I left the interview feeling exhilarated. I want to be an anthropologist when I grow up."*

Throughout the next six months, I followed up on many of the contacts that Roberto offered me; participated in several ChepeCletas tours; re-met other participants in these tours at various other events throughout the city, thus gaining first-hand understanding of the success of ChepeCletas's strategy of getting strangers to meet and see that they share interests; and paid for another fifty-nine cups of coffee in advance for strangers whom I would never meet, but to whom I could feel connected in the community ChepeCletas helped create.

QUESTIONS FOR DISCUSSION AND ACTION

1. How do the goals of ChepeCletas relate to the concerns of your own city or community?
2. Which of the strategies used by ChepeCletas might be effective where you live?
3. What might be the local barriers, in your own community, to such an undertaking?
4. How might you surpass those obstacles?
5. If you wanted to start something like ChepeCletas, who are two or three people you think might help you in such an effort?
6. What might be your first steps for getting started?

SUGGESTIONS FOR FURTHER READING

On the creative city movement
Landry, Charles. 2008. *The Creative City: A Toolkit for Urban Innovators.* London: Earthscan.

---

* In fact, I have been an anthropologist (and a grown-up) for decades. This interview, though, made me feel newly committed to the task and energized me for the next six months of fieldwork.

On deliberate transformation of urban spheres
  Lydon, Mike, and Anthony Garcia. 2015. *Tactical Urbanism: Short-Term Action for Long-Term Change.* Washington, DC: Island Press.
  Montgomery, Charles. 2013. *The Happy City: Transforming Our Lives through Urban Design.* New York: Farrar, Straus and Giroux.
On art, power, and cities
  Rodríguez Vargas, Marvin. 2016. *En la calle y más allá: una aproximación sociológica al arte graffiti.* San José, Costa Rica: Editorial Arlekín.

ADDITIONAL RESOURCES

For more information about ChepeCletas, Pausa Urbana, and related initiatives, visit the following websites:

Permalink for ChepeCletas: https://web.archive.org/save/https://www.chepecletas.com/en/home/.
Permalink for yoamochepe: https://web.archive.org/web/20190529233631/http://www.yoamochepe.com/chepecletas/.
Permalink for Pausa Urbana: https://web.archive.org/web/20190529233811/http://ougam.ucr.ac.cr/index.php/comunidad/buenas-practicas/pausa-urbana.
Permalink to a video about the life of Mr. Robinson: Vargas, Erick. 2009. "ROBINSON: Cuando el Peso Atómico se Difiere." https://web.archive.org/web/20191231023038/https://vimeo.com/21326323.

3

Urban Environmental Sustainability and Gender Equity

In streetwise call and response along a red wall in San José, one graffiti artist corrected another's assertion that "7 out of every 10 women suffer sexual harassment on the street," changing the seven to a ten (see figure 3). The authors of each message – the original and its revision – reflect what Setha Low (1999, 133) asserts, that "spatial arrangements reproduce gender differences in power and privilege." Andrea, the founder of Centro Para la Sostenibilidad Urbana (CPSU, Center for Urban Sustainability), knows this all too well. In her efforts to make San José rival Costa Rica's rural tourist areas for environmental sustainability, she promotes sustainable forms of transportation like biking, walking, and using public buses: anything but relying fully on car culture and the pollution and congestion that accompany it. For this to be successful, she knows that she must also combat the ever-present nature of sexual harassment. Sexual harassment and forms of sexual assault short of molestation or rape share a term in Costa Rican Spanish: *acoso sexual*. This congruity reveals that these phenomena, contrary to their English language equivalents that categorize them as two separate types of unacceptable behavior, represent points along a continuum of aggression disproportionately affecting women. Graffiti in this city reveals that more and more people perceive catcalls as lying somewhere along this spectrum. Spray-painted messages like "My body doesn't want your opinion" and "It's not a catcall, it's sexual harassment" express this sentiment clearly. Andrea recognizes

3 Graffiti indicating that sexual harassment is pervasive for pedestrians

that if people are not safe from objectification and assault when they ride buses or use bike lanes, they are less likely to do so. If safety is heightened because one's own vehicle doubles as a safe space, it will be harder to garner support for other forms of movement throughout the city. As a result, efforts promoting sustainability and the eradication of sexism are linked.

Andrea's view is not merely one of cause and effect, however. Both issues concern her equally, and her recognition of the epistemological value of lived experience, alongside research-based understandings, let the founding leader of the CPSU see these phenomena as intertwined. Andrea is quick to call out all-male conference panels with a hashtag, to draw attention both to the sexism inherent in their organization and to the fact that their composition makes them less insightful. A panel comprised exclusively of male speakers, geared towards decreasing car dependence through advocating bus ridership, biking, and walking, without taking into account the experiential insights of women or gender-nonconforming individuals, might not have seen so readily how sexual harassment and assault might constitute barriers to an environmentalist goal.

For all his brilliance, Jeff Speck, in *Walkable City* (2012, 71, 163; see also Sadik-Khan 2016), acknowledges pedestrian safety from collision with cars as a key precursor to creating cities that urge walking over car use but does not consider safety from gendered violence. If people are simply safer in the immediate realm by taking their own car, they might be more likely to put off the long-term safety of achieving clean air goals. Collaboration with leaders from varied realms of experience and expertise can resolve this myopia. Edward Soja (2010, 199) urges readers to form "crosscutting alliances" in the name of upholding the titular idea of his book, *Seeking Spatial Justice*. Just as ChepeCletas (see chapter 2) partnered with artists from working-class backgrounds to better represent the people who have always used, worked in, and valued the Central Market, Andrea's alliances across various realms of interest demonstrate how seeing beyond a singular issue, and instead understanding how it is connected to other concerns, helps to build more effective solutions.

As with other social movements addressed in this book, Andrea's effort is both grassroots in its application and global in its inception. Andrea is an example of a young leader who drew from global ideas learned in her time working towards a higher education degree abroad, then returned to apply those ideas to the needs of her homeland. In similar fashion, her years working with Global Shapers, a program within the World Economic Forum, both infused her localized successes and allowed her subsequently to further influence a worldwide audience. Andrea's leadership embodies how the interplay between global and local forces moves in multiple directions. Within Costa Rica, following her work with public entities, Andrea came to engage in a sort of entrepreneurial activism by founding a private enterprise, the CPSU, seeking to align the nation's cities with national goals for environmental sustainability. While rural, ecotourism destinations have long succeeded in this regard on a global scale (see Honey 2008; Stocker 2013), the urban sphere has not. As Costa Rica strives to meet its initial goal of carbon neutrality by the year 2021, along the way to the more significant goal of total decarbonization by 2050, Andrea has stepped forward to make sure the capital city does its part.

We met for an interview on the porch of a bustling downtown San José establishment, with a view to the pedestrians and drivers that share a main thoroughfare congested with cars. She ordered passion fruit juice (local, in season), no straw. This offered an apt segue to a discussion about sustainability in the city, and I asked her how it came about that she founded the organization at age twenty-six. First, she studied environmental engineering, as well as topics related to environmental management, climate change, and urban planning, in Costa Rica and in Wales, Israel, Singapore, and Colombia. Next, as part of a public organization, and in response to her nation's carbon neutrality goal, she contributed to the development of a national sustainability certification for urban businesses that was both reliable and compatible with international standards. To do this, she explained, "I had to work with various sectors," and she went on to list government entities and corporate entities, as if in anticipation of my planned interview questions about how Costa Rican social movements appear to differ in this regard from many in North America. Then she added, "but also communities."

Sprinkling English language phrases throughout her speech, she acknowledged that "top-down" processes do not always work. And as for "bottom-up processes," when one starts with communities, it might be hard to get to the upper levels of government or business. But she considered, *"la ciudad es como un punto medio"*: The city is like a middle ground. She developed her organization as a way to offer an avenue through which not only corporations but also urban, municipal governments might apply training they already had in other realms, to themes related to mitigating climate change.

Andrea also valued insights stemming from community-based work. She saw that people in smaller communities were "tired of waiting for the government to resolve [their concerns]." Andrea's idea was to offer an advisory realm through which to support people who wanted to accomplish something for their city, people who might say to themselves, "I want to do something for my community, but I don't know how; I don't know how to apply for funding; I don't know where to start," she explained. She sought a way to lend support to projects dreamed up by "a person who might have a very good idea but who doesn't have a platform from which to seek funding or to develop it." She envisioned this as an office focused on "social action" and "research into themes related to urbanity and sustainability." Looking for models to follow, she identified one from the UK, "to see what was going on outside [of Costa Rica] and see how to apply it here." She added, "I said, 'I want to do this in Costa Rica ... The question is how.'"

In this set of realizations, Andrea's work is in keeping with the understandings of Edward Soja (2010, 144), who recognizes that marginalized groups may distrust the government to act, and instead might opt for grassroots efforts. Andrea Muehlebach (2012, 169) offers an example of organizations that connect social engagement with government, but in a way "in which ethical citizenship operates as a depoliticizing tool while simultaneously opening up new political possibilities." The way that Andrea's philosophy differs from both, however, is in the understanding that government entities can be brought into this process while keeping the issues political, and that her office could constitute a bridge for doing so. Andrea's use of *conversatorios* – solution-oriented, roundtable-style brainstorming sessions inclusive of varied perspectives and potentially opposing stakeholders – engages just this sort of collaboration across various lines of identity and experience. So, too, does her work with university students researching innovative solutions in the realm of sustainability at Costa Rica's Institute of Technology, the public university specializing in engineering. This meeting ground between technological experts and ordinary citizens was part of Andrea's initial goal.

Andrea used money earned through consulting for businesses seeking ways to be more environmentally sustainable in order to invest in studies of sustainability and community projects. This is one way that the business Andrea started reveals that one can generate revenue while working towards an activist goal. In that community-oriented use of profits, Andrea envisioned herself as fulfilling a "social function," "introducing these topics so that these topics leave the realm of experts and become [topics for] citizens." This resonates with Janette Sadik-Khan's (2016, 142) goal of creating "a living partnership between the public and the municipal leaders who serve them to recover a public realm that serves everyone." One way of doing this mirrors Participatory Action Research: a form of inquiry rooted in experiential understandings and work alongside community partners who share equal buy-in and input (see Schensul et al. 2015). Uniting academically based research and grassroots activism to inform her efforts, Andrea's work embodies the notion of praxis, which combines philosophy for social change with deliberate action.

The CPSU offers an effective, collaborative model of problem-solving, linking government offices, ordinary citizens, researchers, and anyone else who might have something to contribute. Eager to work with anyone who has a stake in a given concern, Andrea invites to the table the presumed opposition. Whether convening other social movement leaders, presidents of for-profit bus lines, pedestrians, and the Ministry of Transportation to work towards clean transportation or finding a way to cede portions of already-overcrowded city streets to dedicated bike lanes, Andrea calls for all voices to be heard. Through *conversatorios*, she provides a platform for working collectively and proactively towards a solution.

Taking place after work hours, during volunteered time, sometimes *conversatorios* involve panelists from various sides of an issue, including guests from other countries joining remotely or in person, and an audience ready with questions. At the outset of a given *conversatorio*, Andrea announces that this session is not a place for airing complaints. Rather, it is a salon of sorts, a drawing together of community members to understand varied perspectives on a root problem and develop a solution considerate of all vantage points; it is a guided conversation working towards strategic change. Andrea had the goal that these *conversatorios* "inspire people to do something, that they ask questions, that they see experiences [and examples] from other countries, and that they say, 'I can do that.'"

In this endeavor, she has a successful record. While it is common for New Social Movements to work parallel to government or against it, and, in similar fashion, avoid creating ties too close to corporations, one of Andrea's strengths lies in creating strategic alliances among seemingly opposing sides for the good of the public. Her effort to create an organization that could function as a neutral entity, "that tries to open doors among the three" areas of business, government, and community, is one example of how Costa Rican social movements seem to diverge from many North American ones. The stated neutral position mirrors Costa Rica's official pacifist stance. Following this model, she has moderated solution-oriented brainstorming sessions about varied topics. In one *conversatorio*, differently situated stakeholders met to begin discussions that culminated in the creation of protected bike lanes in a city often deemed too dangerous for cycling. In other *conversatorios*, Andrea has met with varied panelists to address issues related to applying the nation's decarbonization goal to San José. And in still others, the CPSU paired with San José's other collectives and social movements, as well as some activists-turned-artists who painted "guerrilla crosswalks" (see Lydon and Garcia 2015, 8, 13), to observe and promote the Día Mundial Sin Carro (World Day without a Car).

Gathering after the workday, in a memorable *conversatorio* about using bicycle power to drive machines that may serve as resources for local businesses, cycling enthusiasts joined local farmers, business owners, engineers, and the head of a farmers' market popular among urbanites to discuss how a sustainable cacao farm uses bicycle power to produce locally sourced chocolate; to design contraptions to meet needs suggested by the audience, working in teams; and, as a visual-physical-gustatory aid, to try their hand at riding a bicycle-powered blender, mixing sustainably grown dragon fruit into rich, magenta shakes.

In the interview, I recounted to Andrea her own words from the bike-power *conversatorio*: "*Esto no es un 'quéjese aquí.' ... El eje de nuestra organización es de ser híper-positivo*" – This is not a "place your complaint here [session] ... The foundation of our organization is to be hyper-positive." Just as the neutral role of the CPSU mirrors a salient facet of Costa Rica's political positioning, its positive focus reflects another signature characteristic of Costa Rica. I wondered aloud to Andrea to what degree Costa Rica's identity as ranked high on the Happy Planet Index has influenced her model of promoting social change. "Hmmm, *puede ser*," she assented, yet she also acknowledged that hers is not the only model. Movements rooted in protest are also very necessary, she insisted, and they still exist alongside movements that focus on praxis and proactive problem-solving. In fact, she said that the success of past protests based on confrontation rather than on an overtly positive model is to thank for the fact that they are no longer the only way to seek change.

She suggested, "It might be because of how social movements have evolved in Costa Rica. For a long time, [more confrontational social movements] were *very* necessary." She mentioned environmentalist protests that resulted in legislation and "certain guarantees that make it so that it is no longer so necessary" to march. She explained that protests still exist in areas that need more refinement, such as legislation surrounding access to and use of water, and Indigenous rights, and realms that still require people to denounce current practices. She went on,

> But what I don't like about [more confrontational] movements, and with which I have never felt comfortable, is the idea that anyone who is not [of the protesting group] is my enemy. I work with whomever I want to work with. There are mayors that maybe I don't like how they work, but I can work with them so that they work better, you see? ... Maybe I am naïve in this, but I want to be a person who is neutral, a person who supports them, inspires them, and connects them, connects them to citizens ... I want to connect them and build bridges so that things work better.

She continued,

> I think this also comes from the experience I had with the topic of climate change and wanting to articulate a national, governmental policy, but that also had to mesh with [policy used in] the private sector, but for the wellbeing of the nation. So, I had to create something that would work for everyone. The government wasn't going to impose it; those from the private sector weren't going to just do whatever they wanted; but rather we had to create something with which everyone could be more or less content. And that was a first step for the better. People still criticized a thousand things about it, but now we are seeing positive results from it, and it was a first step to get things rolling, because if not, everyone says, "I don't know what to do," and "If I do something it has to turn out perfect," and that is why we are in a state of paralysis as a country, because nobody wants to do anything because everyone will [be critical] if it doesn't turn out perfectly.

She turned back to the role of Costa Ricanness in shaping these perspectives, as she acknowledged that people tend to be critical of people marching in protest or on strike, but the gains Costa Rica has now might exist because somebody protested. Andrea is well aware both that more strident forms of protest in the past are to thank for these guarantees and that they are still necessary for some social issues. Paradoxically, they continue to be a target of criticism from various sectors of the population, across lines of social class, ethnic group belonging, and rural and urban dwelling, just as the legal protection of such protest continues to be a point of pride by some. She suggested that perhaps many of her compatriots are still critical of protesters because "in Costa Rica we don't have anything [of note] to complain about; we don't have such serious problems, so we complain about everything." Andrea laughed as she repeated this observation. She was not the only leader interviewed to insinuate that the safety nets that assure Costa Rican citizens and residents a certain degree of security with regard to food, health, and education (see chapters 1 and 4) allow for this. Of course, there are serious issues to address in Costa Rica, such as those she alluded to earlier in the interview. However, Costa Rica's social guarantees reduce the quantity and magnitude of urgent concerns. Andrea's sustainability efforts are facilitated by the fact that in Costa Rica debates over the existence of climate change are nonexistent. Even opposing stakeholders agree on this, living as they do in a place with pride in its formal commitment to a zero emissions goal. Other Costa Rican idiosyncrasies, such as an overt marketing of happiness and official pacifism, might influence her approach. "It could be. It could be because of that ... I don't like confrontation, unless it is necessary. I am very calm, I try to make peace, to make sure everyone is happy. But when I have to speak up, I do so directly. I try to be diplomatic, but if something has to be said, I say it."

Even then, she prefers to point out what is going right rather than dwell on what is going wrong. Focusing on what the government does inadequately instead of applauding what is going in the right direction strikes her as doing nothing about the situation, and she considers that if she engages in that behavior, "I'm not building anything by being destructive ... The idea is to inspire people and give them a breath of fresh air, you know? ... But maybe being raised in Costa Rica gives me this thing about being neutral, about being positive."

She proceeded to reflect upon an experience she had while living in the UK, where she saw that her behavior differed from that of her peers because she wanted everyone in a social situation to vote, to be democratic in decision-making, instead of one person deciding something for a group. She recognized that as stemming from her formation in Costa Rica. This is an advantage of the outsider perspective. Her experience outside of Costa Rica may well have let Andrea – as well as other leaders who had the opportunity to travel or live outside of their country of origin – see Costa Rican life and possibilities in new ways.

The visionaries of new possibilities who lead the collectives featured in this book began independently of one another, but several have since joined efforts, to lend mutual support, and take stock, collectively, of their individualized efforts. Andrea explained, "One of the projects we have is to see to it that each initiative is doing *something*." She listed the areas of concern such as transportation, sustainability, media, and happiness. There it was again: *"felicidad"* was a deliberate area of work. Collaboration with other collectives fits within her goal of being a connector of sorts, to get areas of identified need to corresponding realms of expertise, because "many times, those working bottom-up don't get to the top levels of government or the status quo." As an example, she brought up the *conversatorio* about making roads safer for cyclists. The vice minister of transportation arrived and heard the questions and concerns of citizenry in attendance, and then asked what his department might do. Subsequent actions following up on those concerns reveal that it was a genuine question. She summarized her role: "Mission accomplished. I connected the community to the person in the position in power. [I created] a bridge of communication." As a follow-up, she acknowledged that she would also like to involve private businesses, "because not everything is the government's responsibility. The responsibility belongs to all of us."

To share responsibility, though, also requires attaining equal representation in leadership. Breaking gendered barriers has been part of her experience. She suggested that women in particular are often taught not to take something on unless it will be perfect, or not to apply for something unless they are 100 per cent qualified, while those same lessons might not be directed towards men. She explained that she was not socialized in the same way and instead opted to engage in activities more often offered to boys. And, she added, she was always "stupidly optimistic." This combination of deliberate ignorance of unnecessarily gendered lessons and adherence to a positive, proactive outlook has gotten results. But she has also relied on support from people who surmounted gendered obstacles before she did. When Andrea first graduated it was a woman who hired her, and she has seen that female students sought out the CPSU for support, perhaps because it is largely women-run. Referring to herself and the co-founders of her organization, she concluded, "We have had very good opportunities and we have taken advantage of them." At the time of the interview, she was planning the Day without a Car event, and she was the only woman involved. "But it has been this way my whole life, so it doesn't make me uneasy."

And yet, discomfort in the public realm – outside of a leadership role – informs her activism. She has been involved in projects to map sexual harassment, to report it, to form brigades against it, and to keep a blog detailing and documenting the ordinary nature of sexual harassment as a facet of urban life that constitutes a barrier to equal enjoyment and use of the city. In years subsequent to the interview with Andrea, these themes would be borne out in graffiti scrawled on major pedestrian boulevards throughout San José. During a march for the Ni Una Menos (Not One Less) campaign on 8 March 2018, a call to action in opposition to femicide, gendered violence, sexual assault and harassment, and other concerns disproportionately faced by women and genderqueer individuals, protesters scrawled messages in an informal aerosol script against the haughty backdrop of historically important buildings and city landmarks. Among those messages was the one noted in chapter 1:

Contra la violencia patriarcal y capitalista
Nuestra alegre rebeldía

Against patriarchal and capitalist violence
Our happy rebellion

As unlikely as it seems that movements grounded in happiness or "hyper-positivity" would be equipped to take on themes of gendered violence, or to mix the two sentiments at all, this is exactly what the youth-led social movements emerging in San José are doing.

Mario, the young leader of Costa Rica en la Pared (Costa Rica on the Wall), an organization mapping graffiti and recognizing it as art, noted in a 2018 meeting that the metropolitan cathedral was quick to paint over graffiti related to the Ni Una Menos protest, whereas even months later, the municipal government had yet to erase it from other buildings of symbolic import. He ventured that perhaps some individuals within the government shared these anti-sexist, anti-violence sentiments, or at least considered them worthy of further contemplation. I can offer no institutional recognition of this claim as it pertains to the graffiti from Ni Una Menos and other graffiti-based critiques of gendered experience in the city. But the ideas they reveal about sexual harassment in the urban sphere have since become part of projects rooted in the highest government office in the nation-state.

Although during our repeated conversations in 2016 Andrea expressed interest in running for the office of mayor of San José at some point in time, and another interviewee insisted that he would not rest until she became president, Andrea had not yet pursued political aspirations. That changed in 2018, albeit in an unforeseen form. That year, she had to relinquish her leadership of CPSU in order to accept an appointment as an advisor to the first lady of Costa Rica, in the newly opened Sectorial Council on Infrastructure, Land Planning, and Mobility. In that role, Andrea's work on sustainable transportation would help shape governmental policy. In this transition, as in all of her work, Andrea's case exemplifies three prominent themes of San José's social movements: 1) it is a movement that is both grassroots and global; 2) it demonstrates the importance and success of forming partnerships across lines of gender and different interest groups; and 3) it holds the promise of engendering institutionalized change.

QUESTIONS FOR DISCUSSION AND ACTION

Andrea knew she wanted to take a model she saw from outside her home country and apply it, but she had to figure out how. Pick a project you have heard about from the international realm as you consider these questions:

1. What is it?
2. How might you have to adapt it to fit your own culture or place?

3. Is there a group already working on this? If so, how might you lend support to it instead of starting a competing or parallel project?
4. Which existing community organizations would be important to include or consult in the planning stages?
5. What are three steps you could take towards enacting it?

SUGGESTIONS FOR FURTHER READING

On the politics of access to space and place

Low, Setha. 1999. "Spatializing Culture: The Social Production and Social Construction of Public Space in Costa Rica." In *Theorizing the City*, edited by Setha Low, 111–37. New Brunswick, NJ: Rutgers University Press.

Sadik-Khan, Janette. 2016. *Streetfight: Handbook for an Urban Revolution.* New York: Penguin Books.

Soja, Edward W. 2010. *Seeking Spatial Justice.* Minneapolis: University of Minnesota Press.

Speck, Jeff. 2012. *Walkable City.* New York: North Point Press.

ADDITIONAL RESOURCES

Another young leader recognized by the World Economic Forum, Monica Araya, offers an explanation as to why a small country like her native Costa Rica might be especially skilled at finding innovative solutions to big issues in this TED talk. Araya also works towards Costa Rica's decarbonization goals, focusing in particular on clean energy.

Araya, Monica. 2016. "A Small Country with Big Ideas to Get Rid of Fossil Fuels." TEDSummit. https://www.ted.com/talks/monica_araya_a _small_country_with_big_ideas_to_get_rid_of_fossil_fuels.

See this talk by Laura Bates about observations regarding the connections among sexual harassment, sexual assault, and other areas of marginalization by gender:

Bates, Laura. 2013. "Everyday Sexism." TEDxCoventGardenWomen. https:// www.ted.com/talks/laura_bates_everyday_sexism/up-next?language=en.

4

Growers' Markets, Local Foods, and Sustainable Business Models

"Eat fruits and vegetables," reads the dialogue box from the mouth of a cartoonish figure emblazoned on a mural painted by Diego Fournier Soto (see figure 4). I mentioned this art to Roberto of Chepe-Cletas, because at first I found it frivolous, given that public art in other major cities often expresses more dire concerns. Roberto suggested that Costa Rica's relative security might lead to less politically charged art. I still entertain this possibility. And yet other leaders have since taught me that eating fruits and vegetables just might be a political concern.

In 2019, Costa Rican news was filled with public outcry at the removal of some fresh vegetables from the list of basic food items that were exempt from taxation in grocery stores, given these food items' role in the staple diet. They would remain tax-free, but without government-mandated price ceilings, at farmers' markets. Growers' markets figure into the efforts of various local leaders towards sustainability. While often this word is taken for shorthand to represent only environmental sustainability, the concept also includes cultural and economic sustainability. One simple way the tripartite notion comes to life in various social movements, collectives' initiatives, socially conscious enterprises, and the local businesses connected to them, is through the purchase of produce directly from farmers at weekly markets common to Costa Rican life. They urge consumers to do the same in order to avoid the excessive packaging common in grocery

4 Mural by Diego Fournier Soto

stores; to diminish the role of intermediaries and instead privilege the role of farmers in the pay structure; and to promote the consumption of seasonal, local foods, so as to cut down on emissions related to transportation of goods from far away. Leaders of San José's social movements have contributed to the chic trend among urban elites to patronize these venues. By promoting weekly markets, young leaders are encouraging a shift in consumer habits by those who can most afford to consume.

This chapter will introduce readers to two contrasting weekly markets and the social class–related observations apparent therein, as well as to businesses promoting the artisanal production of local items, foods, and flavors in a take on nationalism that urges consumer support of working- and middle-class farmers and artists. In particular, the chapter focuses on a restaurant founded and run by Adriana, who enacts a business model that generates very little waste, thereby promoting environmental sustainability; she hires employees who might not get jobs readily, thus furthering cultural sustainability; and she does so in a way that still generates profits, responding to concerns related to economic sustainability for would-be entrepreneurs otherwise interested in sustainability but discouraged by what they perceive as being unprofitable.

In what might be an inverse scenario to that common to North America, farmers' markets in Costa Rica have long been a popular way for working- and middle-class families to stretch a salary, given these markets' tax-exempt sales and customers' ability to bargain there. An orange-red spray of *pejibaye* peach palm or a cumbersome, multi-tiered bunch of green bananas might peek out of the cart a patron brought with them to transport their haul. Tropical fruits of all colors; carrots, radishes, and beets whose giant size would surprise the average North American; and perhaps a white block of homemade cheese, fresh-baked rolls, or artisanal sausage could constitute normal items in a shopper's weekly purchase. This is still the case for the many weekly farmers' markets that dot the urban landscape. Regulars know that they will always get a better deal than at the supermarket, it will involve fewer single-use plastic bags, and if they go late in the day, they can trade choice among a vendor's best produce for a lower cost, so long as they are willing to navigate the crowd, the noise, and smells of fish and meat, which are less notable during morning visits.

In recent years, the popularity among wealthier people that farmers' markets have experienced in North America has been reflected also among Costa Rica's wealthy people. A newer, foreign-influenced, weekly market now offers higher-priced handmade popsicles, smoked fish, fancy pastas, high-end jewelry, and crafts with prices already converted into dollars. Patrons may sit for a spell to purchase luxury foods, many with imported names, or traditional Costa Rican breakfast fare of rice, beans, and corn tortillas newly marketed as vegan and gluten-free. Even its founder acknowledges the good intentions but palpable elitism of the new market.

The difference between the two types of market is marked in various ways, from the asking price for products and the variety of wares themselves to relative numbers of clothing-clad dogs and the vehicles shoppers take to get to the market, whether buses or taxis at one or private cars at the other. The distinction between the two was summed up readily when, on my way to my first visit to the new market, I ran into an old friend from a previous research project. He noted that he had just been to the new market, and enjoyed the social scene there, but was then on his way to the standard weekly farmers' market in a nearby town to actually purchase his produce for the week because it was much more affordable. Whenever I visited the new market, I had the distinct sense that I was "studying up" (Nader 1972): researching the ways of people who occupy higher social echelons and wield more power than the researcher, which runs counter to much of anthropological history. In spite of these differences, at both types of market, shoppers are reducing waste, relying less on intermediaries, and putting money into the local economy by buying directly from producers. This is a value that Adriana, a blogger-turned-restaurateur, has tried hard to promote.

As a young woman, Adriana began her business out of her home, cooking for friends and strangers, inviting them to dinners to meet people. She wrote a blog that encouraged buying produce in season from farmers at weekly markets, and offered recipes for working with seasonal foods. After receiving a grant for women entrepreneurs, she started a small restaurant. Its success led to a larger restaurant, just newly open when I was doing this research. I learned of the place on one of ChepeCletas's tours, the goals of which included getting strangers to meet, thereby making San José friendlier, and to visit local sites, so that Costa Ricans might take pride in their city. Manos en la Masa – a restaurant whose name translates literally to "Hands in the Dough," and alludes to a local refrain akin to getting figuratively "caught red-handed" – was one such destination. I took advantage of the tour to ask her for an interview in the coming days.

When we met for an interview, Adriana was busy getting ready for the day's work. Once she got some necessary chores out of the way, she sat down with a tray of cutlery, paper napkins, and a homemade paste to seal the napkins into which she would roll silverware. Working as she talked, and enacting a role reversal, she spoke the anthropologist's favorite opening line, "*Cuéntame*" – tell me your story. Throughout the interview, the sounds of work punctuated the discussion, often at opportune times, as if offering proof: while discussing the selection of locally sourced coffee, the coffee grinder whirred; while Adriana spoke of her business's success in spite of generous practices that sounded like charity, the cash register chimed; silverware clattered amid discussions of sustainability and reusable implements; and throughout the conversation, her sister and business partner offered sips of coffee to check and perfect the day's brew. Also recurring throughout the discussion were alternating themes of global crisis and local response.

Her successes in Costa Rica were interrupted by worldwide phenomena: diminished funding for an international cooperative for which she worked led her to turn to local applications; economic change rooted in the Central American Free Trade Agreement and its effect on supermarket chains had repercussions for small-scale farmers in Costa Rica. They began to cave to exploitative requirements to be able to sell produce to supermarkets so as to assure that they could sell all of their harvest. Supermarkets, in turn, made shopping more convenient for people who might have found themselves shorter on time than in the past, in accordance with shifts in work culture following North American styles, or with North American companies based in Costa Rica. According to Adriana, "conveniences convert quickly to vice." The two main problems Adriana sees with reliance on supermarkets rather than local farmers are the intermediaries who earn money at the expense of farmers; and the reliance on single-use plastic receptacles. "Convenience generates a lot of trash," she explained. "It generates a lot of plastic that doesn't get recycled. You go and buy a sandwich and a drink and a bag of chips, and you end up with a lot of trash, you know? Lots of fruit that you might buy already cut up, in the supermarket, comes in a plastic container. It doesn't make sense."

In response to this trend, Adriana said, "I decided to work harder to try to reposition farmers' markets: I would go to farmers' markets, I would take pictures, I got to know the producers, and I would interview them. I recommended farmers' markets to people [on social media platforms]; I would share farmers' market hours on my blog, and this would give a little more presence, on social media, to farmers' markets, and then the next step I took was to start a pop-up restaurant in my home." Then came her first restaurant: a small space that shared a building with a graffiti supply store and a non-profit center supporting Indigenous rights, LGBTQ+ communities, and the art scene.

Adriana explained, "I have always felt that in order for a business to be sustainable, it has to be very human." She acknowledged that a business could be environmentally sustainable without considering its treatment of people and community, "but it would [then] be sustainable at the expense of people's dignity, you know?" It could be economically and environmentally sustainable without being culturally so. But Adriana would insist on all three axes of sustainability in her business. "So that is my proposal, that people who visit us get to know what's beyond the food they eat, that they know the providers" behind it. Specifically, Adriana wants to make sure that customers know the people who produce the food they eat.

This was not an instant success. Given that she was not previously educated in all elements of running a business, it was difficult. But Adriana went about identifying the business's needs, the skills required to meet them, and developing those abilities. She described her early days in this process: "At first it was very demanding, very difficult, to make the business start crawling. So, I had to set aside the conceptual part that first year, until we managed to establish our brand, and people got to know us, for our high-quality product. After we consolidated that high-quality product with people's recognition of that high quality, was when I said, 'OK, now I can start to use my marketing strategy; I have to tell people that this product is of high quality for various reasons.' The first reason is that the providers are good providers ... and they have high-quality products." In other words, the primary reason Manos en la Masa has a good product is because they use locally sourced, primary materials that they buy directly from producers. There are no intermediaries. And then business started to grow more and more.

The fact that Adriana could not implement her full vision all at once did not stop her. She started where she could, and then went about enacting her business's philosophy to its fullest – or at least to its fullest as first envisioned. Adriana keeps furthering her goals. Once one step is reached, she strives for more. Guiding each change are her basic beliefs about sustainability and community. As she exchanged her first, small restaurant for a larger one, local media sources helped out, in part drawn to her business because it "had a slightly different business model." Local magazines, newspapers, and print media seemed like a logical extension of her beginnings in digital media and she used these resources effectively.

On this matter, she expressed awareness of how she differed from others who were awarded the same grant funding for women entrepreneurs that she received early on. She described her peers as older women starting microbusinesses. In contrast to them, Adriana came from a position of privilege. She had a formal education, had traveled abroad, spoke multiple languages, and had internet access. Like several other leaders described in this book, Adriana both recognized her privilege and made strategic use of it in order to address social class disparities in the community around her. She used her internet savvy to promote her new restaurant and, in turn, used the restaurant to bolster various sectors of the community. Once established in a larger setting, she said, "We sat down to think, 'OK, we have a bigger place now. Now what do we do?'"

Motivating these concerns were her priorities: "a sustainable supply chain, high quality, and value-added products." The supply chain relates to collaboration among businesses. Where competition does enter into her business model is in pitting her restaurant against convenience stores that rely on plastic packaging for carry-out foods. Manos en la Masa offers food to go – sandwiches wrapped in paper, drinks in glass bottles that can be returned to her, and other snacks that generate no trash. Hers is not the only business in San José to do so: there is already a client base that values this environmentally friendly approach.

Adriana reiterated her goal of "always striving for people to understand that there are different forms of consumption, ways to consume, and that consumption is always a political decision, also." I thought of the mural demanding that passers-by eat fruits and vegetables and saw it with new eyes as expressing a political sentiment. Adriana continued, "And that those of us who have the luxury of deciding what [and how] we consume, should be more responsible with that decision." She elaborated on this idea, noting how and why purchasing patterns may vary by social class: "I understand that people with less income don't have access to what we offer" in Manos en la Masa. "They have to think up ways to feed a large family on very little money. So, obviously, they aren't going to come eat here." Once again, Adriana's awareness of her own privileged position arose. She added that among those families she referred to were farming families. "So," she asked, as if by logical extension, "what can I do to give back, so that the flow of money takes a good path?"

Hers was not a rhetorical question, and she proceeded to outline her response: "I try to guarantee that the majority of the products we use here, the majority of our primary materials, is produced in Costa Rica, in order to enact that distribution of wealth, which many businesses don't do. Many, many restaurants don't do it. There are many restaurants that use only imported products." She listed the exceptions to this policy: olive oil, wheat flour, sesame, and a few other products not generated in Costa Rica. To select suppliers for these items she considers relative distance and the environmental impact of delivery, and weighs that against labor conditions to assure the most ethically sound product available. As always, her considerations of sustainability include environmental factors, human factors, and a form of economics that allows her business to survive. But no one of those decisions should be made at the expense of the others.

In the name of ethical production, she removed some items from the menu. Products known to be cultivated in polluting and exploitative ways – such as pineapple – are not offered at Manos en la Masa. Once again, I thought of the urban art and graffiti scene that is current on such politics. Stenciled throughout the city's walkways is the image of a pineapple and a message comparing pineapple production to the mining industry. While pineapple is grown locally, it cannot be grown on a large scale in a manner that assures the well-being of workers, consumers, and the environment. For that reason, this fruit that is plentiful and nearly ubiquitous on Costa Rican menus is nowhere to be found at Manos en la Masa. And yet, Adriana insists that to uphold her values she need compromise neither taste nor foods that are emblematic of Costa Rican culinary tradition. She offers plenty of other dishes that honor time-worn Costa Rican foodways while filling local cravings.

The menu is not the only area where Adriana enacts her ethical principles. She has considered how she can donate unused space or time in her restaurant to support community causes. She has received university student interns studying food science and gastronomy. She lends a second floor to coworking, meeting space, and entrepreneurial undertakings, charging just enough to cover the expenses of doing so, such as additional staffing, electricity, water, and gas. She is thinking through how she can partner with enterprises wishing to fulfill their stated responsible business plans, to connect donated food with kind-hearted individuals who could use Manos en la Masa's kitchen on its one day off per week to cook food for the homeless. And in lending space to other projects, far from compromising her business, she has found additional time to return to her beginnings in blogging, making the restaurant's recipes available to everyone because, as she explained, "the majority of the recipes were developed collaboratively." Even if she ends up writing a printed book (which would not be her first experience in authorship), she would offer a free, digital version. "We have always had this approach of open culture and open expertise," she offered.

Her blog will also offer a catalog of the producers she relies upon, so that her customers might contact them for their own supply needs; a regional directory of farmers' market locations and hours; explanations of which fruits and vegetables are in season; which are characteristic of a given region and therefore even more locally sourced; and a shopping list tool to help customers decide which products, and how much of them to purchase, at local growers' markets, to prepare a given recipe, also included on the site. She hopes to develop online tools to help people to buy direct and limit food waste.

None of this happens at the expense of her brick-and-mortar business, however. Not only does she offer high-quality food and service to regular customers in her posh restaurant, she also meets community needs. Manos en la Masa participates in the Café Pendiente program (see chapter 5), offering coffee and food to those in need. When a person in search of a free cup of coffee arrives at her restaurant, Adriana treats them as she would any other customer. "Someone else paid, but it's the same service that I have to offer." She indicated the cup of locally sourced coffee she had offered me when we sat down. "For example, if I were serving you a cup of coffee that you didn't pay for, you sit down at a table, and they treat you really well. And why wouldn't I treat someone else that way? Just because they didn't pay, I wouldn't treat them well?" Whether serving a paying customer, an anthropologist invited to a drink, or someone without the means to purchase a cup of coffee, Adriana and her employees offer all visitors the utmost respect.

Adriana explained that after people became aware that she offered both food and respectful service to those in need, whole families began to arrive. Sometimes she prepares packages of food and goods for individuals whom she knows by name, and refers to with titles laden with sincere honorifics, to pick up at appointed times. She began to use her established networks to collect donations of school supplies and gently used clothing to pass along to underprivileged neighborhoods in the urban area. Utilizing her social media connections, she presented the story of someone recently released from jail, to whom an acquaintance donated a suit and other clothing items so that he might be more successful in his job interviews. A few days later, the man stopped by to announce that he had gotten a job. Adriana summarized, "Everyone has dignity and the fact that you don't have money doesn't change that." Yet she insists that her model is not charity: she works to change community.

She cooperates with fellow restaurateurs to find job placements for individuals less likely to get hired. She also collaborates with other restaurants in an agreement to reduce waste. Working with a university student who studied composting, Adriana came to participate in a project that pays a truck to visit various restaurants, collect organic waste already separated from non-biodegradable trash and recycling, and deliver it to be used as compost to one of the farms that supplies her business with produce. "It's like a value-added cycle," she said. She also works with a neighborhood recycling program and strives to produce as little trash as possible: just napkins, items too greasy to compost, and bathroom trash. In these efforts and in her hiring practices and social programs,

Adriana addresses what scholar Doreen Massey (2005, 195) writes about as "the challenge of our constitutive interrelatedness," finding solutions for coexistence within a given space and set of constraints faced by variously positioned actors, brought together through effects of globalization and localization that often play out in uneven ways.

Working to even out such inequities, Adriana reiterated that sustainability includes proper management of waste for environmental reasons and the well-being of her employees, their health, and permission for them to leave work to take classes at the university nearby. She mentioned good treatment not only of people but also of the animals turned into meat. She offered the example of a burger: "If you want to eat a hamburger, eat it, but think about where you are going to eat it, you know? This is what interests us most, that people value the very big impact of their decisions as consumers. Because, if we consume in local markets, and we activate the local economy, and we support businesses that generate work for people who are unemployed, or that have fewer options [for employment], also –" She cut off the thought, turning to the alternative: "There are a lot of big businesses that employ many people that have degrees, that speak two languages. But here, our employees don't have a degree, some are migrants, some speak only Spanish." She pointed to the role of vocational work in diminishing unemployment.

Indeed, San José is the primary destination for urban migrants throughout the nation and for people seeking economic security across borders. "Businesses like this can generate employment for these people, and in so doing, diminish the quantity of poor people, augment the number of people who enjoy quality of life, and even out that balance [caused by fluctuating global economies]. We can help the country be one more centered on local business [than international corporations], because it is more sustainable." Adriana offered a contrasting example. When the country relies on multinational corporations to employ thousands of people, as is the case for many businesses in Costa Rica, sometimes these "do not offer good working conditions, might break laws, and if the company then leaves Costa Rica, it leaves 3,000 more unemployed people. [To the contrary], supporting a local business generates business for Costa Ricans." Adriana added that she is not going to "pick up and move her business to Australia." This is more stable for her employees. Adriana hoped aloud that "many people learn that this is possible, and that they try to do it, too, so that their life generates employment for someone else." She acknowledged that "not everyone is willing to risk everything to start their own business, but for those of us who do, and hopefully every day there will be more of us, we are also generating work for a lot more people who otherwise wouldn't have it, you know?"

As always, when I interviewed inspiring leaders, not wanting to take too much time away from their own goals, I wrapped up the interview, asking what I might do to help. I reiterated anthropology's standards for informed consent in all stages of the research process, and her right to revoke consent or retract information prior to print-ing. "No," she said, suggesting there was no need to review her infor-mation or cut anything. "What I want isn't that people go around saying nice things about me. What I want is that people understand that it is sustainable to do business this way." Coins clanked in the cash register nearby, as if on cue. She wanted to let readers know that "it is a sustainable way to run a business. And it seems like a good idea to document it, so that others learn and say, 'Oh, good, you can do it this way, and it is sustainable.'" She added, noting the restaurant's economic success, "We live off of this. So, I think it is very important that people understand it."

Adriana had answered many of my prepared interview ques-tions before I voiced them, and I was so drawn in and inspired by her ideas that I forgot to ask about the positively focused trend among social movements in Costa Rica. But the question was unnecessary. Her business embodies this proactive stance. This was as true in her treatment of farmers and employees as it was for people in need of food, connections to jobs, or the clothing nec-essary to create a good first impression at an interview. She never did let me pay for my coffee that day. On my way out, I donated five coffees for future visitors in need, and many more throughout my six-month stay and subsequent visits. Each time, I witnessed Adriana enact her spoken ideals: serving food, receiving visit-ing groups, or carrying out the various roles necessary in a small business, always with the same degree of respect for everyone she encountered.

QUESTIONS FOR DISCUSSION AND ACTION

1. Where do you buy produce, and what labor practices lie behind it? How could you find out more about this?
2. How often do your produce purchases involve single-use plastic bags or packaging? What strategies could you employ to mitigate the environmental harm caused by this?
3. Adriana started her project before it was perfectly planned. Instead, she went about adding on elements that fit her philosophy once she had identified and developed the skills needed to carry out other parts of her project. What nascent project idea do you have? What is the philosophy behind it? What skills do you have now that would serve it? What skills must you develop along the way?

SUGGESTIONS FOR FURTHER READING

On food, culture, and politics

Crowther, Gillian. 2013. *Eating Culture: An Anthropological Guide to Food.* Toronto: University of Toronto Press.

Lang, Tim, and Michael Heasmann. 2015. *Food Wars: The Global Battle for Mouths, Minds and Markets.* London: Routledge.

On space and place

Massey, Doreen. 2005. *For Space.* London: SAGE.

On the anthropological concept of "studying up"

Nader, Laura. 1972. "Up the Anthropologist: Perspectives Gained from Studying Up." In *Reinventing Anthropology*, edited by Dell Hymes, 285–311. NY: Pantheon Books.

ADDITIONAL RESOURCE

On the importance of growers' markets

Modarres, Mohammad. 2019. "Why You Should Shop at Your Local Farmers Market." TED Residency. https://www.ted.com/talks/mohammad_modarres_why_you_should_shop_at_your_local_farmers_market?language=en.

5

A Pay-It-Forward Strategy to Combat Food Insecurity

Coffee matters in Costa Rica. In the middle of a busy thoroughfare downtown, a plaque indicates the site of the first coffee plantation; the luxurious National Theater that qualifies as patrimony, belonging to the public, has its roots in coffee barons' colonial-era whims; a public park in the center of San José flaunts hedges made of coffee plants. The bus-ride view from the metropolitan area to more remote areas is rife with hillsides blanketed with coffee planted in tidy rows. In a tasting session in one of San José's many coffee shops, the owner was only partly joking when he fielded a tourist's question about how long he has been interested in coffee: "Since I used to get it in my baby bottle." Multiple afternoons with host families throughout my career have revealed the acquisition of this taste from very early childhood. In the week before writing this chapter, when I sat down for coffee to catch up with long-standing friends and family, one experienced and loving mother in the group softened her baby's digestive biscuit with coffee. The baby had begun learning to recognize the flavor of coffee at four months old and had already participated in the social context surrounding it. When he is old enough to drink coffee out of a mug of his own, it will already taste of family love and belonging. In fact, he received this induction into the world of coffee at his own urging; his mother said she could not deny him this caprice when he reached for her cup.

Twenty-one-year-old Ivannia founded Costa Rica's Café Pendiente initiative upon this idea. She explained, *"El café no se le puede negar a nadie"*: You can't deny a cup of coffee to anyone. Her phrasing reflects the role of coffee as a basic food item and a cornerstone of social interaction in Costa Rica. This beverage, integral to Costa Rica's economy, and the basis of a daily afternoon social ritual, functions as a potent symbol of belonging to the nation (see Tucker 2011 for more information about the cultural, economic, and nutritional realm of coffee). Through the Café Pendiente project, people otherwise at society's margins can participate in the *cafecito de la tarde,* the daily afternoon coffee hour, a brief respite that serves both for sustenance and interaction. Drinking an afternoon coffee offers connection to the nation's history, its agricultural heritage, and its culture. Anyone who cannot afford it merely needs to look for one of the many businesses offering paid-in-advance coffee, as Ivannia's efforts have assured.

In 2012, Ivannia saw a post on Facebook about the Caffè Sospeso program in Italy. She commented to Roberto, from ChepeCletas, that they should enact this program in Costa Rica. Evaluating the situation, she thought, "People complain a lot [as opposed to finding solutions] ... and this happens on a global scale, but why doesn't one just [adopt the idea]? You just have to make the logo and stick it on cafés and announce it and that's it." So that it would not be her alone working on the project, she enlisted the help of ChepeCletas and two other established organizations with which she was connected, if only as a follower on social media. The friends that helped her establish the program were also involved in the same three organizations, which shows how overlapping activist interests may support a fledgling project.

Borrowing from Caffè Sospeso the premise of customers paying in advance for a stranger's coffee, Ivannia developed, spread, and now maintains a program networked across multiple independently owned businesses, in order to offer a way to ameliorate food insecurity in the capital city. Readers from North America might be familiar with acts of spontaneous generosity that include paying for the next customer in line at a coffee shop. The Café Pendiente program makes that sort of friendly gesture more predictable so that people in need might rely on it, as opposed to happening upon it through serendipity. It extends the reach of random acts of kindness by systematizing them.

5 Placard, with the Café Pendiente logo, indicating
that a café has paid-in-advance coffee to offer

A recognizable symbol allows those in need of food to identify participating cafés where they will not be shamed or judged for requesting help. And perhaps because of Ivannia's connections to a social movement geared towards ameliorating the effects of homelessness on inhabitants of the street, as they are known in Costa Rica, the word spread effectively.

A white coffee mug stands out in relief against a round turquoise background, encasing a heart (see figure 5). This emblem, adorning the door or window of many a coffee shop in San José (and, increasingly, in other Costa Rican cities), indicates that it is a business participating in the Café Pendiente program. The number of affiliated coffee shops fluctuated across the span of fieldwork, varying with the relative viability of the small, independently owned businesses that participated. Inside these establishments, printed announcements about the program urged patrons, in a very localized version of Spanish, *"Compartí tu café pendiente:"* Share your paid-in-advance coffee. The *voseo*, a verb form characteristic of Costa Rica and its northern, neighboring Central American nations as well as parts of South America, adds to the community character of the project. Advertisements about Café Pendiente explained, "It is a non-profit initiative that consists of paying in advance for a cup of coffee that someone you don't know, and who cannot buy it, will enjoy." In language use, in content, and through small businesses, themselves working to cultivate local community, the Café Pendiente program invites everyone to take part in a Costa Rican ritual combining nourishment and social belonging.

Ivannia's involvement with other initiatives, including support of refugee populations raising funds through selling prepared foods of their homeland, and her volunteer work delivering services and food to homeless individuals on the street, also attest to this underlying goal. Latin American social movements in the 1980s included taking care to address food insecurity in communities seeking to bring about change in other areas (see Escobar and Alvarez 1992). The grassroots application of a global movement, in the case of Café Pendiente, attends to this same concern, but in a way that is wholly Costa Rican: after all, in Costa Rican custom, you cannot deny a person a cup of coffee. Interviewing Ivannia, I commented that a theme I had seen among the social movements emerging in San José is that they seemed rooted in something other than anger. Ivannia responded, "Yes, I feel that here it is more about wanting to do something good. It doesn't come from anger, so much as from wanting to be part of the solution." Of course, anger as a root cause and a proactive stance can coexist. It is merely that one of these is emphasized over the other in this particular endeavor.

In the name of social science, I purchased coffee at twenty-two out of the thirty-seven businesses either listed on the website or that I identified by the sticker on the businesses' window and donated sixty-one cafés pendientes during my six months of research (and many more in subsequent visits). This allowed me to enact the participant part of participant observation, and also placed me in a good position to talk to owners, baristas, and employees about who receives a café pendiente and how often a free cup of coffee is requested. Some Café Pendiente locations offered apt environments for the seemingly unending task of typing field notes, if I could be sure that occupying a table for a time would not impede their business. This constituted another form of productive waiting (see chapter 1): it positioned me adequately to observe the process of someone requesting or receiving a café pendiente. I also attended two tours co-sponsored by Café Pendiente and ChepeCletas, to visit and learn about three participating coffee shops each time, and I interviewed Ivannia and others who helped to get the program off the ground. These combined methods allowed me to see the individual variations in how the program is enacted, in accordance with the vision of its founder. Ivannia's words reflected the language and goals of appropriation of space echoed by leaders of other projects: "each locale appropriates the concept." Each coffee shop takes ownership of the phenomenon and adapts it to its particular specialty and individual style. Participant observation allowed me to see how this was so and also ascertain how some shops might more readily meet the goal of the initiative than others.

It was easy to envision how coffee shops converted from street-side garages and establishments with large, open windows or entrances along the street, in areas of heavy pedestrian traffic or concentrated homeless populations, might field many requests for donated food or coffee. But other settings seemed less likely to fill a need. Various barriers seemed to exist for some places to deliver food or drink to those who needed them. The metal bars on the door of a coffee shop and the fact that customers had to be buzzed in, would likely prove uninviting to a seeker of a paid-in-advance coffee. The doorbell's very presence might serve as an obstacle to asking for a free coffee. In similar fashion, in a gentrified neighborhood catering to wealthy patrons, the location, itself, might be unwelcoming to those most likely to need a free cup of coffee or a meal. A coffee shop in the heart of the city, set back from the street past a tidy atrium, would require those wanting paid-in-advance coffee to be seen, and perhaps judged, while crossing a courtyard to ask for a handout. And at a café located right along the street, offering local food, coffee, and chocolate, but with French art on the walls, a sandwich board offering *croque madame* in French, brunch and smoothies in English, and exuding music in languages to match, both social class and the languages seeming to encode it might serve as pre-emptive barriers to requesting a café pendiente. While the Café Pendiente initiative might do little to curb larger patterns of exclusion on the basis of social class in these spaces, or their root causes, it did seem to meet individual needs. It offers an example of what individuals and business owners might do to address inequities in the short term that are symptomatic of systemic ills, even as those same individuals might participate in other movements geared towards attending to the underlying causes of disparate access to resources.

In spite of my concerns about various impediments to this program's efficacy, all of these places disbursed already-paid coffee. Multiple baristas at the stylish coffee shop tucked away in a posh neighborhood reported offering free coffee daily. An employee at the shop across an atrium from the nearest sidewalk noted that perhaps they give out fewer free coffees because they are set apart from the street, but still, they do their part. One barista there explained, "Some days they get [no requests], and some days they get a few," averaging out to daily contributions. Sitting often, for periods of time long enough to type detailed notes, in the shop with the locked entryway, I grew accustomed to seeing the same man approach the gate and lean against its metal bars, in a regular ritual of silent inquiry. The cashier would always reach through and hand him a beverage. It was not the most inviting way of distributing food, but it met a basic need, all the same.

In contrast, three coffee shops included in my interviews and observations more actively staved off potential shame inherent in requesting handouts. When baristas saw homeless individuals whom they recognized, they would leave their respective stores to go offer coffee, so that individuals in need might not have to ask for help. Ivannia, in her interview, volunteered additional examples of cafés where this was the case and assured me it was a majority of participating locales that engaged this strategy. Although it required a sole employee to leave the business unattended, it was a tactic I observed while enjoying an afternoon coffee at a shop specializing in hyper-local goods: micro lots of coffee identified by place, purchased directly from growers. Distracted in a conversation with a friend, I was surprised to look up and notice the barista and singular employee, who had served us, emerge from the grocery store across a busy thoroughfare, carrying an armload of rectangular boxes of milk back to the café. He had left the two of us alone, implicitly entrusting care of the shop to us, while stocking up on necessary supplies. This may reveal a level of trust among people perceived to share a community. The inclusive nature of that community extends beyond baristas and patrons known superficially to one another, to homeless individuals, or people otherwise in need, validated as being of that place, rather than as threats to its well-being.

In a similar spirit of community, cooperation among businesses helped lessen the load on any one coffee shop trying to meet needs. A café located right along the street that received up to ten daily requests for free coffee, when they had used up or surpassed the number of donated coffees for a day, would sometimes send those in need to a nearby coffee shop. That other locale's owner and employees, in turn, gladly took on their share of what could be an economic burden for a small business. Although nearby, independent businesses offering coffee might well be competitors, instead they took a collaborative approach.

Adriana, the entrepreneur highlighted in chapter 4, receives numerous requests for assistance. She said that homeless people and the underemployed, itinerant vendors of homemade food, and self-appointed parking attendants guarding cars in exchange for coins are among those who most commonly request a café pendiente. She elaborated, "We don't give money to anyone who comes by asking for it, but we do give food. We give them a café pendiente and something more." She always accompanies the paid-in-advance coffee with food. Adriana and her employees treat those who get a café pendiente there like any other client. She added, "some are ashamed" to be invited in, seated at a table, and waited on like any other patron of her upscale restaurant, but, for the most part, they allow Adriana and her staff to do so. She explained her motivations, "*Tratamos de llevar el café pendiente un paso más allá*": We try to take café pendiente a step farther.

Mirroring the individualized ways in which participating cafés go about participating in the program, ranging from passing a free drink through metal bars, to leaving a shop unattended to deliver coffee to someone in need, or inviting non-paying customers in to take a seat and be treated like any paying customer, businesses also varied in the degree to which they kept track of free coffee disbursed and announced its availability. Ivannia gave up on quantifying cups of coffees given out, because not all business owners record or report it the same way, and some convert paid-in-advance coffees to lunches or protein-rich *empanadas*, depending on what someone needs, and because some participating businesses do not even sell coffee to begin with. One store offers pay-it-forward pizza; another, paid-in-advance cupcakes; and a third gives out blended drinks made of fresh fruit in season. She explained, "The coffee is symbolic, but it can go well beyond that." Even without any form of quantitative proof, though, she saw the program as working. This matched my own imperfect efforts to enumerate success of the Café Pendiente program, while reaching the conclusion that it is doing something.

Although participating coffee shops varied in their reports of how often people request a pay-it-forward coffee, and who received them, certain trends emerged. While a few shops acknowledged people rarely using the program, far more common were responses of "almost every day," "every day," and as often as they had donated coffees to offer. One participating hole-in-the-wall coffee shop run out of a converted garage along a heavily trafficked street noted that they get between eight and ten requests per day. Some cafés had regular visitors, including homeless people; unemployed people or those with few economic resources; underemployed individuals; immigrants in vulnerable circumstances; and, on occasion, someone who might otherwise have no trouble paying for a cup of coffee but who found themself without a wallet that day.

Amid explaining that the majority of recipients are homeless individuals, Ivannia recounted an exception, in which a physician realized, upon trying to pay for his coffee, that he had forgotten his wallet. Embarrassed, he told the cashier he would pay later. Taking a token out of the café pendiente jar, the cashier remarked that it was already paid for. In the face of his hesitance to accept, the cashier explained the program and that on that day, he needed it. The doctor returned later and "paid for a ton of coffees." However, the forgotten wallet scenario is a unique one; far more frequently, those who receive pay-it-forward cups of coffee or donated food on the honor system are people who could not purchase it. This, too, proves hard to record accurately.

A colorful chalkboard at a trendy coffee shop by the train tracks offered an indication, legible from the entryway, of how many coffees were available relative to the number donated. The math did not quite add up. In bright, chalky hues, the board boasted that twenty-two cafés pendientes had been disbursed and five donated, in the two months since the café opened. The one I had just paid had not yet been added, and neither had three others purchased recently, explained an employee. Even so, it was clear that the café would bear the cost of the program in the event that people took advantage of it to excess. At the same time that she countered popular accusations of abuse of the system, the barista offered another qualitative example of success. She volunteered that it is not the same people who pick up a pay-it-forward coffee each day, though she does give one out almost every day. She added that even among the "regulars," homeless people who sleep near the train tracks that lie parallel to this business, and who rely on the program in her coffee shop more frequently, "they don't abuse it." She said that the homeless individuals whom she recognizes as constituting part of her community only stop by two or three times a week, even if they sleep nearby daily, and sometimes when they stop by it is to bring others to get a free coffee or meal, foregoing one themselves. This act of generosity by people who have nothing filled an unforeseen criterion for success that a quantitative evaluation could not reflect.

Exploitation of the system was a common prediction among naysayers, but shop owners – who willingly assume the risk in such cases – overwhelmingly agree the program is a success. They report that community members benefit from this program. While Café Pendiente offers coffee as an entry point, many participating businesses, like Adriana's, also offer food, thus making Ivannia's effort one geared towards combating hunger. And this point is more important to Ivannia than the allegations that people not truly in need might request free coffee. Ivannia explained, "This can't really be measured. We're not going to go around judging who can and who cannot [pay for their own coffee]. So, we base it on trust." Indeed, it is a program that puts trust in humanity, promoting solidarity among city-dwellers, and placing priority on thinking beyond oneself.

Those who pay for café pendiente generally do not see the recipients of their donations or gain any recognition for their charity. Usually, it is a very indirect, private act of generosity, save for the telltale token the purchaser leaves in a jar for the collected coffee beans, buttons, laminated tokens, tamped coffee pucks, or other tangible representation of cups of coffee available for pick up, unique to each café. While most donations are completely anonymous, one coffee shop asked donors to write a brief note on a small, fluorescent sticker adhered to a wall, visible from the doorway, indicating how many coffees had been paid for. Some stickers bore a diminutive drawing of a smile or a coffee cup, while others had uplifting messages, like well-wishes for a good day, a turn towards good fortune, or Costa Rica's signature phrase, "*pura vida*." The pureness of life lived there includes community building. It requires one to care about the well-being of strangers. It calls upon everyone to see their fellow human as an equal member of the community.

In this and other goals, the program did not always work. Yet even its purported failures offer hope. In 2016, a cashier at a participating café in the university town said that they did not get many donors, but if someone walked by and asked for coffee, even if none had been paid in advance, they offered it, and accompanied the cup of coffee with a hearty, multigrain cookie. By the following year, in a return visit, while trying to leave a café pendiente when I paid for my order, a cashier informed me that they no longer participated in the program because people were misusing the system: customers would order and pay for a full lunch in this chic, pricey establishment, and then ask for a café pendiente. This is what the program's critics feared. But instead of allowing abuse of the program, the coffee shop ceased participating; they accepted no further donations and removed the turquoise and white decal, but still disbursed coffee to those in need. Likewise, in 2018, a shop that had been an active participant in the program since its beginning removed its Café Pendiente sticker and stopped accepting donations. Its barista assured me that they still gave out free coffee as needed, upon request, but no longer advertised the program. "It worked, and it didn't work," he said, "*Funcionó y no funcionó*." But even as an example of "failure," this business maintained the spirit of the program.

Most business owners, however, reported greater success. A café owner employing a barista who had himself relied on the program in earlier years, and who donated coffee and time to ChepeCletas and Café Pendiente tours so that more people might learn about the program, encapsulated the sentiment I heard from many: "*La experiencia ha sido muy buena.*" It has been a good experience. Another business owner assured, "It gets to those who need it." As with other facets of this case study, I cannot offer quantitative findings to back this up. It has no ready form of calculation. The program itself requires faith in humanity. So, too, did the study of it. Employees and owners appeared genuine in their appreciation of donations and consistently voiced their support of the program. So, too, did its founder, who knows something about successful contributions to community.

Ivannia's involvement with groups of young people generating change did not start with Café Pendiente, nor does it end there. When she was nineteen, she was involved with a blog about local music, in a place where imported music is the norm. This fits with themes of other movements that bolster the local, and it offered both a platform and ready audience for her nascent blog about Café Pendiente. Café Pendiente, in turn, connected her to other organizations that work towards building community and meeting needs. Just as the more effective Café Pendiente locations seek out people in need, rather than waiting for them to arrive, another organization with which Ivannia volunteers ventures out to fulfill the needs of people on the street who are not, for whatever reason, being served by existing shelters. Ivannia coordinates her part of this larger initiative by finding people who cut hair for a living and can donate their skill once a month.

She also co-leads an urban hiking group that gets people to move through the city on foot, in the name of health, appropriation of public space, and local knowledge. Hikes through a long-standing laborers' cemetery, for example, reveal that Costa Rica has been multiethnic and pluricultural since long before legislation named it as such in 2015. Ivannia's other endeavors include promoting the monthly Art City Tour that gets residents, as opposed to international tourists, to make use of the city's museums and art spaces, for free. She has announced locations for gathering gently used clothing for hurricane victims and used the atrium space in the building that houses one Café Pendiente locale for fundraisers for refugee communities. She has collaborated not only with the movements noted here, but also with the Center for Urban Sustainability (CPSU) (see chapter 3), Manos en la Masa (see chapter 4), and an organization that supports public art. These efforts may not challenge the root causes of the problems they seek to alleviate, but they show what an individual and their respective social network can do to make a difference towards diminishing the symptoms of deep-set social ills too complex for any one person to resolve on their own.

Ivannia's connections to other emerging social movements illustrate how the linkages among these groups make the work of each one even more effective. Contrary to what presiding stereotypes about millennials suggest, she reaffirms that her generation is one that is thinking of others and taking action. In response to my comment about the ties among collectives, Ivannia explained, "Yes, we always try to be like a bridge to help other causes, too." And like other collaborators, she refused to take sole credit for her endeavors. "It's a whole generation," she said. "It's a generation of people that support one another, because, like I said Café Pendiente was born alongside ChepeCletas, and [ChepeCletas] keeps [lending] support. And a graphic designer offered her work for free [to create the Café Pendiente emblem]. Everything is collaborative. We all know each other." These relationships allow them to "help one another and support one another and announce [one another's events]."

Taken together, these linked collectives offer a sort of safety net for vulnerable communities. In contrast to Rodríguez Vargas' (2016, 174) description of whom urban revitalization projects often leave out (see chapter 2), the projects to which Ivannia is connected invite in homeless people, immigrant and refugee populations, and the underemployed. The Café Pendiente program has very few costs (aside from US$5 per starter kit, often covered through donations or tours) and may seem like relatively easy activism, yet it reaches some of the groups most marginalized. In addition to the vulnerable groups already mentioned, many of the participating shops also had stickers alongside the Café Pendiente decal indicating that they were spaces free from discrimination, especially for members of LGBTQ+ communities.

Café Pendiente is an initiative that has been replicated – from the original one in Italy – the world over. It is a project that lends itself well to adaptation in various parts of the world and offers a way for individual donors and businesses of any size to engage in community building. As an expert on social movements Aziz Choudry (2015, 12) asserts, "Movements are made up of ordinary people. Activists and organizers are ordinary people. But ordinary people make change." This is one change that readers might be able to contribute to their own communities.

As enacted in Costa Rica, the Café Pendiente project capitalizes on a symbol of national belonging and economy, and on long-standing cultural norms to meet needs related to food insecurity. Like some of her contemporaries, Ivannia identified a need that was not being fully met by the government, and instead of waiting for others to solve the problem, found a way to make a difference, utilizing the resources she had in the form of social media and internet-based connections. It all started with a Facebook post.

QUESTIONS FOR DISCUSSION AND ACTION

1. Which businesses in your own community might be willing to participate in a project like this?
2. What would it take to get started?
3. What food item would be emblematic of identity or belonging in your community, and why?
4. How might you go about spreading the word?
5. What are some strategies you could use to get such a program known among populations that need it?
6. Which existing organizations might you contact to support, collaborate with, or start a new project?

SUGGESTIONS FOR FURTHER READING

On activism and social movements

Choudry, Aziz. 2015. *Learning Activism: The Intellectual Life of Contemporary Social Movements*. Toronto: University of Toronto Press.

Escobar, Arturo, and Sonia E. Alvarez. 1992. *The Making of Social Movements in Latin America: Identity, Strategy, and Democracy*. Boulder: Westview Press.

On coffee, culture, and globalization

Tucker, Catherine M. 2011. *Coffee Culture: Local Experiences, Global Connections*. New York: Routledge.

ADDITIONAL RESOURCE

For additional information about globalization, economics, and culture as they pertain to the coffee industry, see the film *Black Gold: Wake Up and Smell the Coffee*, produced by Nick Francis, Speakit Films, 2006.

6

Successful Offshoots of a Supposedly Failed Movement

"Can these movements, led by young people, last?" This was a common question in response to descriptions of this research. Chapter 7 will offer one answer to this question, while the present chapter, focusing on an ephemeral collective, offers another. This chapter acknowledges the short-lived nature of one group's interventions, while also noting how its leadership may be poised to make more lasting change. The present chapter aims to demonstrate how a project could still make a long-term difference even if it fails to continue in its initial form. A San José–based group fashioned after a global movement held idea-generating gatherings that, in English, might be called "brainstorming sessions." While the English translation focuses on the cerebral work of finding solutions, the word in Spanish draws attention to the creative process, without dividing the brain from artistic endeavors. Through social media, the collective advertised *"creatorio"* sessions: meetings dedicated to creating. Following various idea-generating activities, the inchoate group of thoroughly grassroots activists set about planning a day full of interventions to get San José's population to think about creating, or perhaps entice them to act upon, positive change. This chapter traces the intervention envisioned by Basthian, an immigrant university student, and first-time *creatorio* participant from the planning stage of his intervention to enactment. It also includes the voices of two of the collective's leaders, urging readers to design active responses to community concerns of their own.

The founder, Randall, explained the transition of various local activists from social movement leaders to municipal government officials institutionalizing innovative solutions. Once-hesitant-participant-turned-leader Yuliana, a graphic artist, spoke of her at-first-reluctant leadership that soon turned to passion. One of them offers the promise of turning youth activism into policy; the other is emblematic of what we know from theoretical accounts of social movement formation: participating in an activity on the urgings of a friend is a common way to become involved in a movement, even for those who never envisioned themselves as activists. Although this movement lasted only three years, its demise is not tantamount to failure. This chapter explains what leaders and participants in a truncated movement did with their activism, beyond the lifespan of the collective that gave rise to it. It also affirms what various scholars (including Fisher et al. 2015; Munson 2008; Engler and Engler 2016) explain about the ways in which activists become involved and how their activism in one realm might engender engagement in another. Finally, this chapter shows how some of the methods of cultural anthropology translate readily to activism and community organizing.

Drawn together by notices published on social media, seventeen strangers and five leaders connected tenuously through real-life peer groups, social ties from San José's public university, and social media gathered for a three-hour meeting in a space lent out for community organizing endeavors. One leader explained that this movement started in Bogotá, Colombia. San José, Costa Rica, was the second major city to take it up when it did so in 2013, followed by other cities around the world. "But," insisted the leader, "it was born here in Latin America." This, too, was a global movement that took root locally. Five leaders, with an average age of twenty-four, divided the session into equal parts. They prompted those gathered – whom leaders referred to as the "grupo motor," a driving force – through a series of thoughtful exercises. Some were activities geared towards interaction among participants, including thought-provoking questions in the fashion of anthropological inquiry, and focus group strategies. Although I had introduced myself as an anthropologist and sought permission to study the session (in keeping with the ethical guidelines of the American Anthropological Association), the leaders made my job easy by following anthropological forms of questioning themselves, keeping questions open enough to allow for unforeseen responses and taking care to avoid leading questions.

One leader began by asking each participant for three words that describe San José. The resulting responses included a hodgepodge of characteristics, some good and some bad: "eclectic," "noisy," "home," "recently open-minded," "traffic jams," "opportunity for change," "survival," "creative," "happiness," "volatile," "cute," "chaos," "culture," and "fast." One person mentioned both "stress" and "peace," perhaps in the same spirit as the person who voiced problem areas as, "opportunities for improvement." Other responses included "a tropical city in motion," "heart of the true Costa Rica," "a nucleus," and, in English, "melting pot," followed by the request to "excuse the Anglicism."

Assorted ice-breaking exercises ensued, involving intellectual, emotional, and physical exchange in various degrees, but always mindful of consent and consensus. At one point, a leader presented an exercise that he said was deliberately intended to make us uncomfortable and to compel us to interact with strangers, as one has to do in cities. Although staged rather than naturally occurring, the underlying idea of this embodied learning strategy for exchange among disparate social groups resonates with anthropological methods, too.

A few exercises later, and after crowding around the small screen of a laptop to watch a brief video focused on happiness in San José, we all sat down again to follow another of the five leaders. He directed us to think about positive and negative things about San José, in no particular numbers or ratio. He gave us all markers and sticky notes. On each note we could write a word. Our task was to "*construir un nuevo imaginario de lo que es San José y construir un imaginario colectivo*": to build a new popular imaginary of San José and build a new collective imaginary. He asked attendees, first individually, then as a group, to consider the elements of San José that they adore. Mentions of well-loved facets of city life, including abundant green spaces sprinkled throughout a crowded grid of exhaust-filled streets, the more-than-century-old Central Market where a long-standing system staves off gentrification even in the face of new popularity, and the existence of so many idealist leaders promoting change soon made their way from participants' lists to bright-colored sticky notes on a wall.

These strengths of the city would be among those tools used to combat items from the other inventory attendees generated: those things that they despise about San José. The acrid stench of urine on public streets; the noise pollution pouring out of speakers set in shop doorways along busy streets at rush hour; and the lack of interaction among strangers appeared as problems noted on papers tacked to another part of the wall. The leader put up categories that leaders had drawn from their past *creatorio* sessions, mirroring the way in which anthropologists draw their categories of analysis from the data themselves, and collectively, we put the adhesive notes in the category where the group – not necessarily the author of each note – thought they might fit best.

Category labels affixed to the left side of the wall constituted negative aspects of San José life, and they included "public transportation," "pollution," "public space," "zombie land" (explained as the tendency of urbanites to share city space without interacting in meaningful ways), and "violence." On the right side were positive categories such as "intelligent space," "climate and landscape," "cultural agenda," "human rights," "situated experience," and "urban culture." Soon, we filled the wall with multicolored papers, situating stress, fast-paced life, and traffic jams in the category of problems with public transportation. Assorted synonyms for dirtiness, numerous specified unpleasant smells, and various terms for noise from sundry sources populated the "pollution" category. "Violence" included child labor in the informal sector, poverty and a rising cost of living, societal indifference to pervasive homelessness, sexual harassment, lack of physical safety, and tension.

On the positive side, the "intelligent space" category encompassed "groups of people who try to change things for the better," "unity and meetings," and "bikes," while notes under the category of "climate and landscape" lauded the city's multiple green spaces and parks. The ever-present idea of appropriation of space and place filled the column under "Cultural Agenda," as did "abundant nightlife," "art," "diverse identities," "history," and "urban culture." "Unity," "sharing," "love," "peace," "a right to work," "diversity of religion, ethnicity, gender, and sexual orientation," and "inclusion" filled in the board under the label "Human Rights."

Then we metaphorically stepped back to see the larger picture, like an anthropologist would after gathering data. On the negative side there were thirty-four notes; on the positive side, forty-seven, and one in the middle. In further good anthropological form, a leader followed up on the divvying up of phrases into leaders' preconceived categories to ask what was missing. Suggested topics included housing; disorganization; planning; a category for inequality (into which "housing" could be placed); and mistreatment of animals, which some said could be added to the "violence" category. The informal economy could be added to a category on inequality. Once "drugs" was changed to "drug abuse," it moved from its temporary position between the two poles to the new "inequality" category on the negative side.

A leader explained it was our job to design interventions in order to counter one of these problem areas, perhaps using the positive elements as strengths or skills to bring to the task. We would carry out all of these interventions and more on a specified day, scheduled for three months later. One leader pointed out that, for example, the previous year's participants put a bed and a toilet under a bridge to draw attention to the fact that people live on the street. He related this to the sticky note that mentioned the "stench of urine" to show how an intervention idea would speak to a problem noted on the board. Then, referring to the spate of problems tacked to the wall, a founding leader asked, "What problem will you own?" He expressed the hope that participants would come up with 100 distinct, symbolic interventions to carry out on the designated day to leave the space better than they found it.

For the remainder of the *creatorio* session, we met in smaller groups to design interventions. Then to close the meeting, a founding leader urged us all to "appropriate this initiative as our own," or bend it to our own uses. Another leader reiterated, "This sense of appropriation" is one idea of the whole movement. I wrote in my field notes that the entire activity, on the scheduled day of interventions, would act as an appropriation of space and place, and as one giant act, or perhaps a conglomeration of multiple, small acts, of emplacement.

Basthian, a university student who initiated one small group in the *creatorio* session, paraphrased his professor when he suggested that one can reach people through various means: one can do it through "happiness," as one option, "but what reaches them better is a clash [*choque*]." The interventions designed that day and carried out months later followed both strategies. Basthian would use conflict as a springboard, while Yuliana would focus on happiness as a point of departure.

A few days after the *creatorio*, I met with Yuliana for an extended interview. Like the other leaders showcased in this book, Yuliana breaks stereotypes of millennials that frame this generation as uninvolved or apolitical. Yuliana's case asks us to upend that particular stereotype and reframe another. An additional stereotype of millennials criticizes a perceived unwillingness to conform to a standard work environment. Yuliana's experience urges us to see that in a more positive light: her distaste for nine-to-five jobs left her creative space and scheduling to engage in community building. Her efforts with the collective constitute only one example of that.

In a more-than-two-hour interview, Yuliana explained how she came to participate in the collective. Like many activists (see Munson 2008, 49, 52, 55, 63; Fisher et al. 2015, 56, 58, 59, 67, 86; Engler and Engler 2016, 150), Yuliana did not envision herself as an activist; she got involved because a friend wanted to go to a meeting. In the end, her friend did not attend, but Yuliana did, and there, she made more friends. That first year, Yuliana designed and carried out an intervention, making origami animals out of recycled newspaper, in a subtle statement about two concerns: reusing resources and animal rescue. Sitting in a public park, next to the city's iconic statue of John Lennon on one side and a kind, chatty stranger on the other, that moment led to meaningful interactions and in-depth discussions with people previously unknown to her. Thereafter, she went from being part of the *grupo motor* to the leadership team, tasked with logistics, permissions, and finding sponsors. She saw her role as that of a facilitator, connecting one participant to others, leaving each one to "begin to act of their own accord, not waiting for the government to solve things." She asked, rhetorically, "If I can do something on my own, and organize it myself, what's stopping me? Nothing. Only me."

In this sentiment, Yuliana's call to action echoed that of Andrea (see chapter 3), but while Andrea created a platform to connect citizens with government, Yuliana's was more of a DIY approach. And just as some of Yuliana's ideas ran parallel to Andrea's, others resonated with those of Roberto (see chapter 2). Yuliana noted that one of her objectives was to "change the mentality of people who are afraid to walk around San José, or who don't like San José, or who have never dared to change their route and have not discovered the beautiful places that San José has." She continued, "There are too many people who have not visited San José for years, for those reasons, out of laziness, fear, or because it has a negative connotation." She went on to recount how, through her involvement and contagion of love for the city, she was able to change the opinion of a friend, again in keeping with what various scholars (Munson 2008; Engler and Engler 2016; Fisher et al. 2015) teach us. Yuliana sought to bring about a change in perspectives on San José by lightening things up. She mentioned joke-telling interventions done on buses to relieve commuters' stress, and jugglers at intersections performing in the carefully calculated, time-limited space that traffic lights allow, entertaining drivers, without slowing them down. In contrast, Basthian used a different avenue.

On the day of the *creatorio*, I joined Basthian's breakout planning session, in the name of participant observation. His suggested intervention stemmed from an assignment from his university art class. For a prerequisite to his art major, in a group project assignment, he had to create public art – be it a mural, an intervention, performance art, or digital art. His group developed a project that they called #TodosSomosDiferentes that had a performative aspect and a corresponding digital platform. At the time, he was merely doing homework; he did not identify as an activist. As of a follow-up interview in 2018, he still did not identify with the label "activist," though he recognized that his interventions had become more frequent and that many would consider them activist. His intervention in 2016, as in subsequent years, involved individuals standing together in public spaces holding large signs on which they both owned and contested stereotypes people held about them.

In 2016, along a pedestrian boulevard crowded on weekends, a young man held a sign asserting that being atheist did not make him less human. Next to him, a friend's sign instructed that being religious did not make her ignorant. A young woman wearing a short skirt demanded that her form of dress did not invite evaluations of her physical appearance. A young man indicated that being sentimental did not mean he was weak, and a woman held a sign noting that women can be strong, too. While a gay man's sign attested to his masculinity, not lessened by his sexual orientation, a woman's sign explained that not having children did not make her any less of

6 2016 intervention by #TodosSomosDiferentes, in which a young
activist holds a sign indicating that his immigration status
does not constitute a burden to the state

a woman. Basthian himself held a sign insisting that his status as a
Nicaraguan immigrant did not mean the state pays for his existence
in Costa Rica (see figure 6). A man passed by, giving him a thumbs-up
and shouting, "Brother!" acknowledging their shared experience.

People going about their business on Saturday stopped to talk to
sign-holders, debate with them, or offer a fist bump in solidarity. Others read the signs aloud to children. Strangers interacted, in accordance with one goal stated at the *creatorio*, to combat "zombie land,"
and individuals confronted stereotypes. Most people walking past
read signs, glanced briefly at the face of the person holding the sign,

then moved on, reading the next sign. Even if they did not stop to talk to the sign bearer, they did not merely walk by, pretending not to see.

Part-way through the intervention, our group was joined by *Habitantes de la Calle*, an organization comprised of homeless people and their supporters, holding stencils messed with paint in the negative space image of messages that appeared along the boulevard that day. They declared, "the city belongs to everyone," in deliberately gender-inclusive language, and other phrases urging city-dwellers to recognize the homeless among them as part of their community. One read, "I exist." "Things happen," said another. The message, *"perdón,"* called passers-by on their discomfort at the presence of a homeless person by begging their pardon, in a phrase equivalent to the "excuse me" uttered when two bodies collide unintentionally. Another stencil, seemingly directed at the street inhabitants, reassured, in local parlance, *"sos importante"*: you're important.

While the intervention was a success in that it got strangers to interact and to question stereotypical assumptions, the collective that prompted it, perhaps, was not. The group did not continue. And yet, as in the case of Café Pendiente participants that stopped advertising the program (see chapter 5), this failure is anything but. Although neither Yuliana nor Basthian considered themselves activists, both have persisted in their efforts to bring about change, based on views and strategies they developed through their participation in a nascent movement. Randall went on to volunteer his time to convene several collectives once a month to see how to collaborate effectively. In 2018, Yuliana was combining social media and video platforms with art, broadly defined, to draw more young people to Costa Rica's public universities. Short video broadcasts focused on *artivism*, identities, Indigenous realities in Costa Rica, and innovative business proposals developed by women. She was still working with the underlying strategy of identifying a need, considering the strengths she and her community had to offer, and pairing them to generate positive developments in society. I caught up with Basthian in 2018, also. He ducked out of his sculpture studio at the University of Costa Rica in order to meet me over coffee. Of the five leaders involved in his first effort at enacting #TodosSomosDiferentes, three remained active in the project while pursuing their respective university degrees in the realm of art.

Since 2016, they had made some changes. They adjusted the name of their project, now #SomosDiferentes, to be more gender-inclusive by dropping a word which, by grammatical default, implies maleness. But the project itself continued largely unchanged. In the past year, they had enacted more interventions than in any previous year, hoping to challenge stereotypes prior to a contentious presidential election in which matters related to LGBTQ+ rights and immigration, among other topics, emerged as key issues for voters. The #SomosDiferentes project would allow undecided voters to interact with people bearing identities often stereotyped – immigrant identities, LGBTQ+ identities, a sign identifying someone as having had an abortion – and invite questions and respectful discussion. It could offer a forum for people to actually meet someone embodying the labels batted around in political debates. Other art-related projects Basthian had taken on in recent years included some that drew attention to homelessness and one regarding the appropriation of space and place. As we spoke, he told me about a project he was developing, linking photography, the telling of people's personal histories, and a goal to connect people who might see one another as strangers. All of these themes resonate with those addressed in the *creatorio* session two years prior.

Randall, the primary leader of that session and series of interventions in 2016, also continued to act in accordance with the goals of the collective, albeit in a different sphere. In 2017, working for a municipal government, he stood poised to institutionalize some positive changes. In the *creatorio* session, he explained to me that some of the leaders of other collectives had taken on government positions. One founder of ChepeCletas was working as the vice minister of transportation, and another as the vice minister of housing. Institutionalizing the goals of ChepeCletas and like-minded collectives could make significant changes in San José and in Costa Rica. However, it will be neither seamless nor quick. Even in 2016, Randall warned that there are changes that take place, from social movement leadership to governmental leadership. *"Te absorba la institución mucho. Tu prioridad cambia."* The institution absorbs you. Your priority changes. Working within government bureaucracies, there are more people to say "no." In social movements, he explained, "people act until someone tells them 'no.' But in the public sector [in government work], people don't do anything unless they know someone will say 'yes.'" The realm of government presents more limitations. And yet, I remain hopeful that young leaders transitioning from social movements to formal government will endure the slowness of bureaucracy to bring about change, nonetheless.

Even though the social movement that called for 100 interventions challenging problems plaguing the city did not endure, the spirit of it did. The individuals involved in it continue to embody the ideals expressed by leadership of that initial movement. In 2016, an explanation on social media explained these as the movement's underlying beliefs:

We believe

- In action over opinion
- That it is possible if we work, imagine, and create change together
- In local actions to generate global change
- In the possibility to create new histories and new realities

In varied forms, the leaders and participants in this movement continue to enact these beliefs. Moreover, they exemplify what literature about social movements tell us about how and why people get involved. Fisher, Svendson, and Connolly (2015, 58–9, 77, 82) and Munson (2008, 49, 51–2, 63), writing, respectively, about movements whose constituents might well be ideological opposites, reach the same conclusion: it is people's social ties, more than their individualized sets of beliefs, that spur them to get involved in a social movement. Yuliana first attended a meeting because she wanted to hang out with a friend who was going (in keeping with Munson 2008, 49, 51–2, 63). Basthian became involved as an offshoot of a school-related project (following the assertions of Munson 2008, 52, 61; see also Kirshner 2015). Once there, each of them began to develop further their ideological stance (in accordance with Munson 2008, 20, 30, 44, 66, 195). Engler and Engler (2016, 150) agree: "A common misperception about nonviolent action is that it is necessarily focused on touching the heart of the opponent and leading to a conversion. In fact, the impact of sacrifice can have little to do with changing the views of one's adversaries – and much more to do with affecting one's friends."

The leaders showcased in this chapter also uphold another assertion made by scholars of social movements. Fisher et al. (2015, 83, 86,

117) explain that once involved in social movements, individuals are more likely than the average citizen to get involved in civic engagement or government. Randall, the convener of the *creatorio*, supports this view, as do other leaders of social movements noted in this chapter and in chapter 3. Through his efforts to convene various collectives regularly, he also exemplifies what Fisher et al. (2015, 59, 70, 82) clarify about how those involved in some social movements are likely to link to others as well.

As a result of these connections to other movements, and also people's social ties, we can see proof of Munson's (2008, 44) claim, "activism emerged [in the lives of Munson's interviewees] not because they consciously sought it out to express their beliefs but as an unintended result of their ordinary lives. The organizations and relationships they have in their lives – and especially at times when their lives are dramatically changing – are the key to the mobilization process." This rings true for the participants in this collective, and in their lives following its disintegration.

While this chapter offers an example of a supposedly failed initiative, albeit one whose successes endure, the following chapter offers an example of sustained activism, over the long term and in spite of sizable obstacles. To conclude this chapter, however, and in alignment with Randall's call to action, I ask, "What problem will you own?" And turning the insights and rhetorical questions Yuliana asked herself to you, I urge readers to "begin to act of their own accord, not wait for the government to solve things ... If [you] can do something on [your] own, and organize it [yourself], what's stopping [you]? Nothing. Only [you]."

QUESTIONS FOR DISCUSSION AND ACTION

This chapter invites readers to replicate the organization's *creatorio* brainstorming strategy to identify a community's strengths and needs, then find innovative ways to apply those strengths to the service of meeting their own communities' needs.

1. What are three negative characteristics of your community?
2. What are three positive characteristics of it?

3. In what ways might you engage the positive elements – strengths, skills, or characteristics – to mitigate the negative ones?
4. Neither Basthian nor Yuliana identified with the term "activist." What does the term "activism" mean to you? By your definition, to what degree does their work fit? How does it pertain to you?

SUGGESTIONS FOR FURTHER READING

On social media–based activism
> Bonilla, Yarimar, and Jonathan Rosa. 2015. "#Ferguson: Digital Protest, Hashtag Ethnography, and the Racial Politics of Social Media in the United States." *American Ethnologist* 42 (1): 4–17.

On how people get involved in social movements
> Engler, Mark, and Paul Engler. 2016. *This Is an Uprising*. New York: Nation Books.
> Fisher, Dana, Erika Svendsen, and James Connolly. 2015. *Urban Environmental Stewardship and Civic Engagement: How Planting Trees Strengthens the Roots of Democracy*. New York: Routledge.
> Kirshner, Ben. 2015. *Youth Activism in an Era of Inequality*. New York: New York University Press.

ADDITIONAL RESOURCE

See the following talk about placemaking in cities:

Montgomery, Charles. 2014. "The Happy City Experiment." TEDxVancouver. https://web.archive.org/web/20191231030300/https://thehappycity.com/project/the-happy-city-experiment/.

7

LGBTQ+ Activism in the Long Term

Whereas preceding chapters attend to social movements led by young people, this chapter responds to questions regarding what happens when leaders grow up and the extent to which the project they started might grow with them. This chapter demonstrates that collectives like these can sustain themselves in the long term, in spite of the struggles with burnout common to activists' experience. While this chapter highlights don Marco, a leader who is not a millennial, it revolves around a topic that continues to be a concern for millennials as well as for Gen Z. Decades before he would age into the respectful title "don," used for addressing elders, Marco began working in a movement to promote rights for gay- and lesbian-identified individuals in Costa Rica during an era when homophobia was an overriding social theme of the nation-state and the cultures that constituted it. At age seventy-three at the time of the interview in 2016, as president of the LGBTQ+ group known as Movimiento Diverso, he contemplated the changes the movement had undergone during his years of involvement, growing more reflective of the varied stances and concerns of differently positioned LGBTQ+ community members. Don Marco offers an example of staying power, demonstrates strategies for sustaining a social movement across time, and offers specific advice to allies.

I sat down to speak with don Marco on a Saturday afternoon at the time he reserves, each week, for meeting with students who seek him out to ask questions for their university projects or other individuals wishing to interview him. He invited me into his home and we spoke over coffee, along with three university students who arrived at his regular session. There, gathered in the living room, this affectionate and friendly grandfather shared with us the origins of his social movement as enacted in Costa Rica, the changes he has seen, the obstacles his group faces, and its successes.

While he is not a young leader himself, don Marco volunteered his approval of them. He confirmed that "youth are very committed," and explained the role they played in a successful "Diversity March," the name for what in North America would more likely be called Pride. The march had happened early in my research trip, and I had vivid memories and photos to match his description. Gathering early in the morning were several floats with banners in English and Spanish and a few participants and allies milling about. Loud music came from a float decorated with colorful fans, bearing a banner from a multinational corporation and the tourism industry. Those vendors who might normally sell a Costa Rican flag at a patriotic parade merely exchanged their wares for rainbow flags. A snack vendor pushing a ramshackle wooden cart scraped an enormous block of ice with an old metal scoop, in order to fashion the same snow cones with sweetened powdered milk and colorful syrups as always. The parade route was just getting set up. It smelled of cityscape, as usual: some garbage, some rain, traces of urine, and lots of people.

T-shirts bearing prideful messages and oilcloth banners from doctors' and lawyers' associations seeking to depathologize LGBT identities joined the scene. Along the sidelines, stood a trans woman in traditional Costa Rican folkloric dance attire, the *traje típico*, with the skirt's standard white, blue, and red ruffles exchanged for rainbow colors. "*Sí, amor,*" came her kind, baritone reply to my request for permission to take and post her photo. The march's appropriation of space was similar to what I saw in other social movements, and this woman's ownership of national symbols resonated with equally appropriative acts within this march.

At the head of the parade, just behind the municipal band's sousaphones, lent for the occasion, after the white-gloved hands fingering clarinet keys, and a band intoning the city's welcome, performers on stilts, just like at any *tico* parade, interacted with the crowd. They wore green parrot and scarlet macaw costumes, reflective of Costa Rica's ecotourism draws, and they performed as golden eagles, evocative of the nation's pre-Colombian riches; they dressed as treasure. Again, symbols of *patria* asserted this group's belonging in the nation. This time, police stood protecting the marchers from people along the route, rather than the other way around, as in years past. A tide had turned. Following the band came the mothers, to whom this year's parade was dedicated. A well-known cookie company donated bright yellow shirts with red letters spelling out the company name and the messages of marchers: *Yo <3 mi hija trans; Yo <3 mi hijo gay.*

Then came the marchers. Hours of them. Thousands of them. They marched in pride, some in drag, many bearing signs, supported by governments and embassies, political parties, NGOs and transnational corporations, families, friends, universities, nightclubs, and academic clubs. At the end of the parade, the crowd dispersed. The next day, its participants might go back to not holding hands in public, not displaying affection, and the supportive allies might return to silence on the matter. The signs would be destroyed or put away, the feather boas stored, and the banners folded for the next year.

Don Marco reported it had been the largest parade ever in the history of the nation, 45,000 people strong. It was not always this way, however. The first time they held a Pride march, seven years earlier, only thirty people attended. The following year, 1,000 people participated. From there, it kept growing. Likewise, the Diversity Movement has grown incrementally. Don Marco explained the movement's origins: "We started because of AIDS," at the end of the 1970s. With a corresponding rise in homophobia, the group became more active, especially as institutionalized queerphobia caused increasing danger for LGBTQ+ communities. Being a gay man in Costa Rica was a crime until 1977. A change in law thereafter did relatively little to stop extralegal forms of pressure and punishment, however. Even once queer identities were no longer penalized, intimidation tactics and social pressures remained.

In the mid-1980s, under the pretext of forcing HIV testing, police rounded up individuals perceived to be gay. Concerned community members took out a full page in the newspaper decrying this as a violation of rights. The ad ran on 5 April 1986, and this became the moniker of the nascent organization: the April Fifth Movement. Primarily, this group promoted education surrounding safe sex practices.

7 Front of a decades-old landmark of LGBTQ+ presence in the heart
of San José. Given the degree of homophobia still to be fought
in Costa Rica, as elsewhere, this chapter is devoid of visual
images of the Pride march, in which people might be identifiable.

Later iterations of the movement followed the community's changing
concerns.

In the 1990s, community members knew that police entered gay
bars more often than other establishments. "They came out of morbid curiosity," explained don Marco, "but behind that morbid curiosity was repression." Bar owners at one of the first gay bars in San
José (see figure 7) took to switching on a yellow light by the door
to alert patrons when the police were on their way in. Prompted by
the light, same-gender couples dancing switched to hetero pairs, or
left the dance floor altogether. Police would round up gay couples,
shave their heads, and publish a list of people, outing them, in a major
national newspaper known for salacious headlines. Some of those
outed lost jobs; some lost family. Those who were financially able to

do so might leave the country until their hair grew back, so strong was homophobia and its corresponding social repercussions. But don Marco explained, one day, "people organized, and said 'we're not switching on the light anymore.'"

Discrimination against gay and lesbian individuals still exists, but don Marco insists that the group most discriminated against is the trans community. "I don't know a single trans person who has not been kicked out of their house," he said. "They have gone about conquering a space" for themselves in society, "but it's not complete." At the time of the interview, trans individuals could be photographed on their national identification cards in accordance with their own gender expression but were not yet able to change their name on identification cards from their given name to one that better corresponded with their gender identity. The Diversity Movement was engaged in a long fight to assure that an identification card could actually come to accomplish the task for which it exists. Given that these discriminatory practices have their roots in governmental institutions, it is no wonder that early on, don Marco and his contemporaries had to work against the government, in the movement's beginning.

Then, his views likely resonated with those of activist icon Angela Davis (2016, 35): "I don't think we can rely on governments, regardless of who is in power, to do the work that only mass movements can do. I think what is most important about the sustained demonstrations that are now happening is that they are having the effect of refusing to allow these issues to die." But in recent years, don Marco found support in government. For the Pride march in 2016, the municipal government lent their band and police force in support rather than withholding the former out of protest and using the latter to intimidate marchers, as in years past. In other realms, though, he has continued to work to change government policy and practice, especially through its legal system. In a necessary paradox, he is using the legal system in order to change it from within. In contrast to earlier years of the Diversity Movement and its precursors, don Marco now counts on support from individuals who have made it into government, biding their time and developing their careers in spite of obstacles against LGBTQ+ community members. In those earlier years, it had to have been difficult to spark a movement built on hope. But as Angela Davis (2016, 29) notes, "Sometimes we have to do the work even though we don't yet see a glimmer on the horizon that it's actually going to be possible."

Through a combination of hope and action, members of the Diversity Movement have made various changes in the collective since its early years. For one thing, it has gone from working against government to working alongside and through it. Its leader has, in relatively recent years, operated similarly to other leaders of social movements in Costa Rica, willing to work with like-minded entities. As with others in this spate of small, youth-led *colectivos*, the Diversity March, unlike New Social Movements in the Marxist sense that organized around social class identities and in opposition to government and capitalist enterprise, was open to collaboration with government entities as well as transnational corporations and private businesses rather than working parallel or counter to these. They did so in cases where they were all striving towards a common goal and they did so with a proactive agenda.

It is understandable to question rainbow capitalism, but the organization had its reasons for engaging with it, however cautiously, in 2016. Assorted transnational giants, not emblematic of shared goals of promoting the local but aligned in their views of inclusiveness, joined the Pride parade route with rainbow messages of acceptance, while local businesses did not always smile upon the LGBTQ+ community within their neighborhoods. It is the transnational corporations that overtly boast hiring practices inclusive of the trans community, although don Marco named only one that he has seen follow through on this claim. While there are companies in which employers insist that they are open and respectful of all gender identities, thus assuring fair hiring practices, don Marco noted that discrimination in hiring, as in housing and education, still abounds. While readers in North America may be skeptical of the corporate motives of these march participants, for now, the inclusion of transnational corporations within the Diversity Movement's annual parade may constitute a tactical, ephemeral alliance, or what Margaret Kovach (2009, 129), writing about a different context, might call a "strategic concession." This is but one approach among many employed to further the overall goal of acceptance and inclusion of LGBTQ+ communities. It remains to be seen if this tactic will continue, but it is appropriate to value the expertise of don Marco as well as his nuanced understanding of the particular constellation of constraints reigning in Costa Rica, both at that specific moment and within historical context.

This history of changing strategies as needed to further a goal reveals the shifting nature of the cultural landscape on which the movement is enacted. The gains the Diversity Movement has won came about through a combination of consistent, deliberate work across decades, and also relatively recent influencing factors, like social media. Don Marco assured, "Mass media and social networks have played a very important role in favor of our movement." Yet in spite of new forms of media to help the cause, traditional obstacles remain.

Don Marco described the primary barriers he sees as being products of "patriarchy's chauvinism and obligatory heterosexuality." Reiterating for the students present at the interview a basic introduction to cultural anthropological understandings of gender as a cultural construct, don Marco explained, "what is feminine and what is masculine is cultural. [We know this] because there are other societies [around the world] where what is [deemed] feminine and what is [considered] masculine is different." Indeed, variety in gender identities abounds cross-culturally (see Nanda 2018). The same is true for human sexuality, its multiple manifestations, and the way that cultural context shapes expectations surrounding these. Don Marco explained how Costa Rican culture, its emphasis on patriarchy, and its connection to organized religion exerts pressure over gay men's expression of sexuality.

By means of illustration, he offered, "One man falling in love with another is an affront to patriarchy, and to machismo." To explain how this came to be, he said, "the first insult a gay boy hears is to be called *mujercita*," little woman. "This is evident in houses, schools, families, public transportation, streets, bars, and in religion." Before the students or I could ask a question, he clarified, "Religion comes from the development of patriarchy. It is not that religion created patriarchy; rather patriarchy created religion. These are the principal obstacles," in Costa Rica, an officially Catholic nation-state, where religious beliefs directly influence law. Young people and some individuals of don Marco's generation alike are clamoring for a division between church and state. In the meantime, though, while changes have occurred in politics, that realm's infusion with one organized religion, within a government meant to represent a religiously heterogeneous population, presents significant barriers to change.

The president in office at the time of the interview made notable advances for LGBTQ+ communities. Underlying then-president Luis Guillermo Solís's policies, explained don Marco, were strong social movements urging change. The most noteworthy changes brought about by the Solís presidency included some symbolic actions and some that became codified into law. Mr. Solís was the first to raise the rainbow flag over the Presidential House. This performative act signaled other, more tangible, advances. His administration passed Executive Decree 38999 in 2015, legalizing rights for same-sex couples in many realms, though ultimately stopping short of marriage equality. His government enacted an anti-discrimination law and spurred consultation with the Organization of American States regarding lesbian and gay couples' rights and legal name changes for trans individuals. Also, by law, public school teachers became required to include curricula regarding sexual diversity. Don Marco's hope is that this institutionalized change within education can prevent adolescent suicides, the majority of which in Costa Rica are rooted in intolerance for LGBTQ+ identities. Yet these advances still leave room for change. Don Marco explained that the primary objectives for which his movement was fighting were fivefold.

The organization strove towards marriage equality, and don Marco and his partner don Rodrigo's case was in Constitutional Court, the highest court, awaiting ruling. At the time of the interview, the Diversity Movement was also working on legislation regarding gender identity so that trans individuals could have their gender identity reflected on citizens' identification cards. Don Marco's organization was drafting proposed legislation on hate crimes so that discrimination would be criminalized in educational realms as well as those related to housing and employment. The Diversity Movement was also pairing with the national Ministry of Health to devise a protocol so that heterosexuality would not be an assumed default for patients, and so that health care – a point of pride in Costa Rica – could be more fully available to citizens and residents. This goal also includes making sure hormones and other needs of the trans community are covered by state-sponsored health care. And finally, just as the Diversity

Movement had its beginnings in the early era of HIV, HIV-prevention continues to be a reigning concern.

Don Marco was quick to point out that, contrary to persistent popular stereotypes, HIV is not a "gay disease," but the gay population is disproportionately affected by it, including among homeless populations. For this reason, and because intolerance for LGBTQ+ identities may result in young people being forced to leave home, homelessness within this community continues to be a concern for the movement's leaders. Don Marco's group strives to make sure that shelters can house and treat HIV-positive homeless people, whether they are citizens or undocumented immigrants. Don Marco also works in conjunction with the Ministry of Health to keep up with advances in antiretroviral drugs and ways of treating HIV involving fewer pills to be taken daily, so as to facilitate the likelihood of homeless populations being able to store medications disbursed monthly by the national health care system. In this goal, don Marco is collaborating with the appropriate governmental entity to seek realistic solutions under the current constraints of the health care system and of realities lived by homeless people.

Don Marco enumerated these five goals, reiterating, "These are the priorities we have at this moment." Since the time of the interview, he has seen some successes. With regard to the goal of marriage equality, Costa Rica's government essentially ran down the clock, delaying any decision until passively giving way to the Inter-American Court of Human Rights' 2018 demand for marriage equality in all of the OAS member states. Through this mix of national and global efforts, marriage equality is slated to become law by May 2020. By more active means, the Diversity Movement reached the goal regarding identification cards accurately reflecting trans individuals' gender identity in 2018. The remaining goals are still in process, as is the Diversity Movement's overarching endeavor. As don Marco expressed the concept underlying each one of the Diversity Movement's projects, "the most important part of all of this is to earn respect." He clarified quickly, "Not tolerance – because that means 'I can withstand it' – but respect. To share and to learn. Once one learns [about LGBTQ+ communities], le nace el respeto," respect is born of this process.

But while don Marco remains optimistic, not all of his comments were tinged with hope. Ending the interview, he toggled between

stories emblematic of success and those marked by tragedy. He spoke
of the original author of the April Fifth newspaper ad demanding fair
treatment who is now a respected judge. He told us of a trans woman
studying theology, poised to become the first trans Lutheran pastor in
Costa Rica. But with voice breaking, he also told us of a nine-year-old
gay child who died by suicide after being evicted by his homophobic
parents. And don Marco had just received word that, in a town far
from the capital city, a fourteen-year-old struggled with the homophobic acts of his parents, his mother standing in his bedroom daily to
pray away his sexual orientation. Don Marco spoke of so many young
people no longer welcome in their homes or families, many of whom
are likely to be preyed upon in the urban realm. Just as don Marco
revealed these contrasts, he was quick to note what the organization
is doing about it; the Diversity Movement is never passive, neither in
the face of positive change nor heart-wrenching problems. Don Marco
was engaging his network to find a more progressive family to take in
the teenager so that he might be able to continue his studies and not
end up on the street.

Then don Marco returned to more uplifting news: a traditionally
conservative municipality had just elected a trans woman leader. This
would not have been possible even five years earlier. In a parallel gain,
he reported that at the moment, 51 per cent of Costa Rica's population
accepted rights for lesbian and gay couples, whereas fifteen years ago,
71 per cent was homophobic. "That's a good social change," he summarized. He went on to illustrate what he called "a broad change in
mentality."

One day, not long before the interview, he complained on social
media about a stranger driving by who identified him as the leader
of the Diversity Movement and stopped the car just to shout insults.
Immediately after posting his frustration, don Marco ventured out.
Several more cars stopped, also to let him know they recognized him,
but not to offend. Most were strangers, or, at best, mere acquaintances.
They honked the horn and shouted, "Keep going!" "We support you!"
"Gay people shouldn't be discriminated against!" and "Good work!"
In total, just after venting on social media about one driver stopping
to say rude things, four drivers stopped to offer encouragement. One
added, "So that you see that cars don't only stop to insult you." On
other days, people have approached him to let him know that because

of him and things he has said publicly they have changed their views or accepted a family member identifying as part of the LGBTQ+ community. People will tap him on the shoulder on a crowded bus, to verify that he is the leader of the Diversity Movement, acting with a certain reverence, as if meeting a celebrity.

He added, as if in cautionary warning not to overestimate the importance of these gestures, that this is how people treat him, a cisgender elder, and a known member of the community; he is aware that this neither erases nor counteracts hateful acts and comments that other LGBTQ+-identified people confront. And yet, these interactions have led him to start counting, literally, the acts of kindness and hateful comments he hears. For every single insult he hears on the street, there are thirty affirmations of appreciation or encouragement. "For every person that insults me, there are thirty who support me," he concluded. For this reason, don Marco is hopeful. And yet, his is a measured hope.

Don Marco invites us to see the positive changes afoot but not become complacent in their presence. His is an active hope; it is a hope to be engendered. He works towards it assiduously and encourages all of us to do the same. When students asked how they could support his efforts, he offered advice for lending solidarity. In universities, he said, always try to include sexual and gender diversity in every club or organization. Speak to these concepts and include them actively. Attend Pride marches, whether or not you identify as LGBTQ+. Participate as a group outwardly asserting support of LGBTQ+ communities. My own observations of the Pride parade and life as it was lived the next day along the same parade route urge me to emphasize his first piece of advice: include support in everyday moments, not just extraordinary ones.

The surge of support visible on the day of the Pride march was all but erased the next day. The day after Pride, few businesses still had a rainbow flag visible. The day of Pride had been a spectacular success. But it was just a day. The day after Pride, homophobia marched onwards. The snow cone vendor would return to selling to a childhood crowd. The flag sellers would go back to the usual *bandera tricolor*. The court case would trudge forward, slowly, plagued by delays, blocked by religion and conservatism, in spite of the tens of thousands of onlookers, maybe even some who felt it was festive on one day of the year to support LGBTQ+ compatriots but not the stuff of year-round displays. The next day, Paseo Colón and Avenida Segunda would be open to traffic again, dotted with Costa Rica's signature red taxis bearing yellow triangles on the door; it would again be filled with the sound of honking horns and city bustle, of a capital going about its business. The rest of the days of the year, don Marco continues to pursue his Supreme Court case to be able to marry legally his already husband. He grows older, not at all the image of the young people on parade.

Where the Diversity Movement differs from the majority of collectives included in this book is in its leadership. While the other social movements emerging in San José were created and led by hopeful millennials bringing global ideas home and applying them in grassroots ways, the Movimiento Diversidad has a septuagenarian leader, who weathered the years when police intimidation was the norm yet was willing to work with police after their sudden shift. He lived through years when the government shamed anyone found during surprise raids on the few gay-friendly nightclubs in San José, shaving their heads and printing their photos in national newspapers, so that they might lose jobs, friends, and family. He remembers well the years when the yellow light at La Avispa bar would warn of an impending visit by police, and people dancing switched partners to stay safe from such intimidation tactics.

Whereas the vibe of young leaders in other *colectivos* was refreshing, inspirational, and energetic, that of this leader was different. It was restrained yet steady. His was not a sprint. He would need to mete out time and energy in a way that could last. I wondered, of the young leaders' efforts, if their burst of vitality could endure, if it could be sustained across the years of growing up, pairing off, and maybe raising children, in keeping with family and social pressure. This remains to be seen. But the Movimiento Diversidad shows what happens when a social movement grows up: it keeps battling. It may have occasional bursts of energy and happiness – parades, even – but much of the work is quieter, constant, and perhaps less joyful. Still, the Diversity Movement's leader remains cautiously positive. Don Marco sees the progress made in his lifetime and notices that it has accelerated of late. He counts the displays of support he witnesses to prove to himself and others how many times over they outnumber the hateful looks, gestures, scrawled messages, and threats.

This is how the other movements may end up, too: less eager perhaps, but still hopeful, opting for proactive work over despair and persistent in their efforts to change the world. Like the other social movements examined here, the Diversity Movement, too, draws from global trends and adapts them to local needs. It reflects LGBTQ+ rights activism from other parts of the world, and applies it to the local environment, rallying around crisis points such as the peak of the AIDS epidemic in the 1980s and continuing forward since. It does so amid threats and violence, promoting pride, consistently, across time.

Initially, don Marco was a reluctant leader. He took action because it was necessary and accepted a leadership role because someone had to. In chapter 5 we examined the role of ordinary people becoming leaders, in keeping with what Choudry (2015, 12) had to say. In similar fashion, Davis (2016, 66–7) encourages us to take heart in the "fact that ordinary people adopted a critical stance" as needed in the space of social movements, even within "social realities that may have appeared inalterable, impenetrable, [that] came to be viewed as malleable and transformable." Don Marco offers us one such example. Across the thirty years of his involvement, he has had to adjust strategies in order to adapt to cultural changes around him. But this is the case for any long-term movement. Through efforts both grassroots and global, don Marco and others within the Diversity Movement work towards his goal of respect through sharing and learning so that respect might be born of its own accord.

QUESTIONS FOR DISCUSSION AND ACTION

1. What surprised you about don Marco's experiences and strategies? What does this reveal about potential cultural differences and similarities between his generation or community and yours?
2. What do you know about LGBTQ+ rights movements in your own region? How do you think they compare to the obstacles faced by don Marco, his solutions, and his continued struggles?
3. What do you think about rainbow capitalism, the prominent role of transnational corporations in Pride events?

4. Don Marco outlined some simple ways for anyone, regardless of gender identity or sexual orientation, to lend solidarity. What are some ways you could put his advice into action in your own university, clubs, or the extracurricular organizations of which you are a member?

SUGGESTIONS FOR FURTHER READING

On intersectional activism

Davis, Angela Y. 2016. *Freedom Is a Constant Struggle*. Chicago: Haymarket Books.

On LGBTQ+ political and activist history

Faderman, Lillian. 2015. *The Gay Revolution: The Story of the Struggle*. New York: Simon and Schuster Paperbacks.

Gould, Deborah. 2009. *Moving Politics: Emotion and ACT UP's Fight Against AIDS*. Chicago: University of Chicago Press.

Haritaworn, Jin, Ghaida Moussa, and Syrus Marcus Ware, with Río Rodríguez. 2018. *Queering Urban Justice: Queer of Colour Formations in Toronto*. Toronto: University of Toronto Press.

On diversity in gender identities across the world

Nanda, Serena. 2018. *Gender Diversity: Crosscultural Variations*. Long Grove, IL: Waveland Press.

ADDITIONAL RESOURCE

On LGBTQ+ activist history in recent years

Richen, Yoruba. 2014. "What the Gay Rights Movement Learned from the Civil Rights Movement." TED. https://www.ted.com/talks /yoruba_richen_what_the_gay_rights_movement_learned_from_the _civil_rights_movement.

8

An Invitation to Action

The case studies presented here share several common characteristics. Most are youth-led and all are solution-oriented, proactive, and collaborative. They are attentive to gender equity and inclusive with regard to social class, ethnicity, sexual orientation, and physical ability; they are intersectional. These initiatives promote the appropriation of space and place for all members of a diverse society. They contribute to movements that are global in impetus while implementing grassroots applications in response to local needs. They prove that it is possible to take on a big issue with just a small group of committed people. The connections among these collectives are conducive to mutual support. Finally, these movements are artful. Some elements that helped give rise to their success – such as the relative smallness of Costa Rica and cultural norms that make it easier to gain access to personal contact information for leaders and interested participants – may not work so well in North American urban hubs. Yet the social media platforms that spurred supportive linkages among these collectives are likely to be equally effective in readers' own communities. This chapter reminds readers that one benefit of ethnographic inquiry away from home is that it teaches one not only about the culture studied but also provokes reflection on one's own culture. The present chapter invites readers to bridge those considerations with insights and tactics from the collectives described here in order to plan their own grassroots-and-global movements at home. To further encourage the application of urban Costa Rican leaders' approaches in other settings, this chapter presents a brief discussion of successful implementations of some of these strategies outside of San José.

Throughout six months of ethnographic research in 2016, I traveled back and forth between the city and my long-standing field site, Chorotega Indigenous Territory, where I worked on other inquiries, visited family-like friends, and carried out service projects. Although courses in grant writing and research design advise against taking on more than one study at a time, I found that going between two field sites meant seeing each project from within and then taking a step back, translating it for another audience, and listening to questions that arose. Doing so allowed me to analyze each project from another angle. In a beneficial way, this dialogue intensified the iterative nature of ethnographic research. This movement between sites also left room for serendipity.

While a great deal of planning goes into ethnographic research, happenstance can also play a crucial role if an ethnographer lets it. On a day off spent introducing a friend to a favorite mural I learned about through research, we got caught in the rain. And rain in Costa Rica is serious business. When the sky breaks open, making talk inaudible, it leaves an anthropologist awash in waiting. Readers may recall from chapter 1 that researchers can put waiting to good use. On this day, the rain was too much for our umbrellas to handle so we waited out the storm under the narrow awning of a business near the painted wall we had sought. In Costa Rican Spanish, there is a word for the time spent waiting out the worst of a rainstorm; a business owner uttered it when he invited us in from below the awning. Chatting there about what we were doing staring at that particular wall led to a conversation through which the business owner offered to connect me to the artist. Through the rain, the three of us talked about the teardrop inscribed, unmoving, on the rain-slicked face of a child painted on the mural (see figure 8). This was not a display of happiness. The artist, Hein_Uno, later explained that he wanted viewers to know that not every childhood is happy. His work urged passers-by to attend to hunger, abuse, racism, or whatever other ills might be lurking in a seemingly happy city. And yet, while not happiness-focused, like that of other leaders, Hein_Uno's work is proactive.

8 Mural by Hein_Uno

The fortuitous rainy-day connection to Hein_Uno, and the understanding that art can prove useful in projects aimed towards social engagement, served the interests of a youth group in Chorotega Indigenous Territory. In my anthropologist-as-culture-broker role, I bridged the two realms. Following phone calls, grant-writing,* and meetings with youth, local government, and a Peace Corps volunteer to sort through the concerns of variously positioned stakeholders; subsequent to youth-led community bingos to raise matching funds and frenzied purchase of graffiti supplies; and after a missed bus and waiting time that turned to an invaluable history-of-San-José-graffiti tutorial, Hein_Uno, the urban art expert, and Mario of Costa Rica en la Pared (see chapter 3), accompanied me to Chorotega Territory, several hours from the city. This application of urban strategies to a rural realm included a collaborative workshop on identities and representation; instructional sessions on *autogestión* (a blend of self-determination and management); lessons on anthropology, Chorotega Indigenous history, and Indigenous art in Latin America; and tutorials on contemporary muralist and graffiti art technique. Following this process, Chorotega youth designed and painted a mural reflecting their vision of their place in the world, their history, their present, and their community.

Just as it was possible to adapt urban art-related research connections to my rural field site, with the support of Indigenous leaders and community members I also applied the Center for Urban Sustainability's *conversatorio* model to local concerns, by convening a storytelling session the likes of which had not happened for years but that had been a hallmark of contemporary Chorotega life for the elder generation. Likewise, I followed the underlying idea of the Art City Tour (see chapter 2), which aims to offer greater access to museums and galleries to Costa Ricans as opposed to foreign tourists. Inspired by that effort, I joined my urban and rural connections to orchestrate a field trip for Chorotega community members to see the archaeological objects of their own heritage housed far away, while facilitating connections between community leaders and museum officials for future ventures in autonomy.

---

* The Guanacaste Community Fund provided a generous grant for this project.

The adaptation and application of strategies learned in the city to a rural realm with different cultural underpinnings and stakeholders allowed me to understand these social organizing techniques from the inside. This in turn led to additional connections and further insights. By translating and extending the strategies of urban leaders to rural life, I was able to test how well they might be adapted to different places, cultures, peoples, needs, and identities. By taking these approaches out of the environment in which I had seen their success, I could scrutinize their respective abilities to bring disparate parties together and work collectively towards solutions acceptable to multiple and potentially opposing sides. They were effective. They served community needs and also anthropological inquiry (see Sanjek 2015 for additional ideas about why this combination is important, and for varied case studies on carrying out such "mutuality"; see Kovach 2009 for related considerations in working with Indigenous communities or as Indigenous researchers). This etic approach to learning the strategies used in San José's collectives, combined with an emic implementation of them, enriched the research process and product. The mural project in Chorotega Indigenous Territory, in particular, seemed an apt capstone of embodied learning.

Days later, when I departed Chorotega Territory and returned to the city, readying to leave Costa Rica, I had to add to the already difficult and long list of goodbyes to people a saddened leave-taking of the murals and graffiti around San José. My field notes for the day read, "Walking around, I feel like I will miss the graffiti, and seeing its changes. Oddly, it feels like anticipating missing a person. I reflected a little on ChepeCletas's and other urban goals, and realized they worked: I grew to love this city." The field notes conclude, "I walked home, thinking of heartbreak and place." These pieces of public art had been key informants, of a sort. I had gotten to paint alongside their artists by means of participant observation. I had watched one wall change from vibrant canvas to painted-over blank surface, to vandalized wall, to funded project run by a gatekeeper muralist and his contemporaries. In that last stage, symbols of Costa Ricanness – an oxcart, local species of flora and fauna, and corn – took center stage in azure, cerulean, and cobalt. Just as these painted emblems are key to Costa Rican senses of self, I had witnessed muralism itself as a type of placemaking and appropriation of public space become central to

San José's identity. I stopped to photograph the semi-circular array of blue-stained brushes, artful even in their resting state, drying in the sun while their owners took a break. Following the click of the camera, I looked up to see and greet the renowned artist and graffiti supplier who helped coordinate the Chorotega mural project.

In studying cultural phenomena, an ethnographer also plays a role in them. We should neither overstate this influence nor ignore cultural anthropologists' potentially meddlesome practice; we are not mere bystanders. Cultural anthropology involves community engagement. We can see this in the bridging of communities, the extension of networks, the applications of ideas from one sphere to another, the use of our anthropological skills and knowledge to seek funding and support for community projects, and the dialogues that enrich each realm. Ethnographic work is iterative: it folds back in on itself, with the ethnographer's nascent understandings informing the way of studying that which they document. It brings into dialogue emic and etic views, putting both to work. And just as the leaders of movements used foreign ideas to adapt to local needs, one of my next steps, in addition to publishing this research, is to think about which of their organizing strategies could work in my home community.

But at the same time that a designated period of research comes to an end, the concerns studied continue, change, and adapt. Any study is, in this way, inherently incomplete. The case studies in this book represent a moment in each collective's history. In the time between research and publication, a contentious presidential election took place and hinged, in part, upon discord surrounding LGBTQ+ rights and marriage equality. A millennial candidate, representing an inclusive agenda, won. On the day of his inauguration in May 2018, he arrived at the ceremony in a hydrogen-powered bus, the technological innovation of which was designed by Costa Rican physicist and astronaut Franklin Chang Díaz. The bus bore the name *Nyuti* – a Chorotega-Mangue word for star, representative of a long-gone language, forcibly ousted upon colonization.

Leading the motorcade were citizens on bicycles, emblematic of the new president's sustainability goals. The presidential sash – symbolic of leadership over a varied and divided populace – was handed over by a student who identified as trans. The head of the legislative assembly – a woman – spoke of inclusion, human rights, and the commitment of citizenry to do their part. The vice president, an African-American woman, seemingly offered proof of inclusivity to a country too-familiar with racist exclusion. The symbols of this ceremony embodied a stated presidential agenda that very much resonated with the goals of the organizations presented in this book: making public space accessible to people from all backgrounds, a focus on environmental sustainability, and affirmation of LGBTQ+ communities.

Not only were their goals represented, though. So, too, were some of their leaders. Among the bike riders were members of groups interviewed for this book, representative of social movements in the urban sphere, who sought ways citizens could make a difference. One of them would leave her post as leader of a collective to take up a new position, hired by the first lady, to tackle matters of sustainable infrastructure and urban mobility. Just as it was a *traspaso de poderes* – a democratic transfer of power – from one president to the next, it was also a transfer of social movements from their grassroots birthplace to their institutionalization within formal government.

How these changes or the president's campaign promises play out remains to be seen. The same is true for all of these social movements. Just as people asked frequently, "What if the leaders of these movements grow up and move on?" (as discussed in chapter 7), critics often voiced the concern that these collectives might neither last forever nor create permanent change. My response might seem flippant, but I offer it in all seriousness: "So what?" Even if they do not endure, they have already contributed to society. Leaders identified a need and set about puzzling through what they might do about it. If the only solution we entertain is a perfect one, guaranteed to succeed and be lasting in the long run, change will be elusive. Instead, we can study a situation and see if there are already groups working on it. If so, we can lend our support to them rather than beginning a rival project. If not, we can consult varied voices and stakeholders, act thoughtfully, take in criticism with an open mind, adjust and adapt accordingly, and move forward.

Andrea, the leader of the Center for Urban Sustainability (CPSU), highlighted the importance of surpassing fear of criticism (see chapter 3). She noted that to get started, a project need not be flawless. Instead, one can look at it as "a first step towards making things better." Of course, Andrea did thorough research before diving in, but even then, when criticisms arose, she addressed them, made changes, and kept working. All the while, she stayed focused on being proactive, until the movement she started reached the precipice of creating institution-alized change. So, too, did Randall, former leader of an initiative that lasted a mere three years.

While the collective highlighted in chapter 6 did not continue, it served as a springboard to leadership and it offered a platform for development of the nascent #SomosDiferentes project. It also included participants from other social movements, such as a café owner that participated in Café Pendiente, an artist promoting consumption of local goods, and an individual who networked to mitigate homeless-ness. One of its leaders built upon tentative alliances among collectives that arose through social media. Following up on such networking, Randall spearheaded a monthly, face-to-face gathering where lead-ers of San José's various movements could report on their plans and projects, avoid scheduling conflicts, and foster cooperation and collab-oration. What began as a loosely based network on the internet trans-formed into a social network in real life. Other connections among social movements also proved mutually beneficial.

ChepeCletas and Café Pendiente often combined efforts, sometimes alongside Manos en la Masa. Among Café Pendiente locales were sev-eral places that also identified as spaces free from discrimination and friendly to don Marco's efforts with the LGBTQ+ Diversity Move-ment. Café Pendiente's leader worked closely with the leader of an organization attentive to issues related to homelessness. ChepeCletas advertised the Diversity Movement march on its calendar, promoted the Art City Tour, and networked with various artists, alongside Pausa Urbana. ChepeCletas's way of seeing how streets invite or prevent biking and walking also made its leaders aware of accessibility for disabled individuals, thus fomenting another area of collaboration. ChepeCletas's goal of steering away from over-dependence upon cars meshed readily with the goals of the CPSU, and both collectives coop-erated on the observance of World Day without a Car.

ChepeCletas and Café Pendiente both devised solutions to bridge social class divides and to direct wealth and disposable income to individuals and businesses with greater degrees of need. The CPSU's *conversatorios* convened ChepeCletas, the farmers' market leaders, and other organizations with shared goals. Both in real life and through social media, these collectives lent support and strength to one another. In this manner, small-scale volunteer initiatives, group efforts, social enterprises, and small, for-profit businesses with activist goals, individually and in concert with one another, supported a variety of social movements. Taken together, these case studies offer multiple success stories. Even through the example of a so-called failed movement, we can see that the end of a given collective is not tantamount to a lack of success. To the contrary, it might indicate growth.

Randall's strategies, as well as those used by Andrea, Yuliana, and their respective co-leaders, resonate with the methods of cultural anthropology: seeing a problem from multiple angles, listening actively to varied views, and translating concerns across different interest groups. So, too, did the tactics used by the artists involved with many of these projects. The artists connected to the collectives described in this book – be it tangentially, as graphic designers (such as for Café Pendiente; see chapter 5), or directly, as leaders and thinkers whose artistic training taught them to seek creative solutions (like Basthian and Yuliana, in chapter 6) – also have something to teach us.

Like anthropologists, artists may see a problem from multiplex vantage points, holistically. We saw this in the metal curtains project (see chapter 2), where artists utilized experiential understandings from their own social circles and social class backgrounds to be sure to include those members of a community who might otherwise be displaced from a newly revitalized downtown area. In efforts to appropriate space for the public, the artists and project leaders deliberately thought through how to make sure that public space was, indeed, available to all. As they claimed space in the city, the muralists of San José painted life around them, drawing attention to social concerns as well as to the country's beauty and symbols of identity (see chapter 1, chapter 4, and the present chapter). Indeed, as Arlene Dávila (2004, 192–3) informs us, murals are "important places of memory, vesting their authors with the role of 'cultural workers' and community artists." In turn, the collectives that favored local production valued the work of local artists (see chapter 4). And artists, too, offered strategies for seeing differently, offering an apt metaphor for the methods of cultural anthropology.

During his leadership of the Chorotega youth mural project, in order to see his work from relative distance, Hein_Uno shook the spray paint can he held in hand and leaned back at a sharp angle from the wall where he painted burning red eyes on a jaguar. He explained to the young artists in his newfound, temporary crew that while attention to detail is important, an artist must constantly step away from the close-up, detailed view, to take in the bigger picture. Anthropology urges us to do the same: attend to local concerns, and their larger, global, context. This tacking back and forth between near and distant perspectives offers a complete view (see also Elliott and Culhane 2017 for more ways that anthropologists can draw from artists' techniques to enrich anthropological inquiry). It is an approach used by the young leaders, also, as they adapted global programs to local needs (see chapter 5), or found regional solutions to worldwide problems, such as environmental sustainability (see chapter 3).

Artists can teach us about strategic alliances, short-lived or not, that may be engaged in the name of meeting a goal. While readers of chapter 7 may question the participation of corporate entities in the Pride march and criticize the tendency to work with rather than parallel to or against government, here, too, we have something to learn from the artists. Artists have long had to balance the sort of work that feeds a soul with that which feeds a family. This entails sometimes engaging in work that pays monetarily but is less fulfilling artistically. They also have to confront accusations of selling out for doing so. They may align themselves temporarily with employers, thus facilitating the financial means to then further the work that they find more meaningful. So, too, might leaders of other movements.

The strategies employed by (mostly) young leaders showcased throughout this book offer possibilities for engagement. These techniques need not be used instead of marches and protests and they do not have to replace movements that use outrage as a wellspring for strength and collective action. After all, moral anger is justifiable and can serve as a powerful driving force. Movements rooted in it have been necessary and gave rise to the importance of attending to intersectional solutions, a point of departure shared by the collectives in this book. Rather, the strategies highlighted here can coexist with ways of creating change that people might be employing already in their own community. They offer additional possibilities for spurring social change. They might allow activists involved steadily in more wearying forms of protest to take an emotional break, while staying engaged, by drawing alternately from varied emotions as different sources of motivation. Or they may be complementary. As Andrea showed us (in chapter 3), the tactics highlighted here might be used to expand upon gains gleaned through protests or marches. Consider these approaches part of an arc of possibilities from which to select in combating a given social ill. To this end, I urge readers to identify a concern in their own community and consider which of the strategies outlined here – in isolation or in conjunction with others – might lend itself well to that issue and to a reader's own skill set, social networks, comfort level, or leadership style. In conclusion, then, I ask readers to turn the ethnographic lens and potential for activism to their own communities, urban or rural, North American or rooted in another part of the world, as you consider the final set of questions.

QUESTIONS FOR DISCUSSION AND ACTION

1. What are some of the salient concerns of your own community?
2. Which of the strategies used by the groups described in this book might lend themselves best to your community's concerns?
3. What steps might you take to attend to gender equity, and a diverse and inclusive leadership and participation base with regard to race, ethnicity, age, social class, immigration status, sexual orientation, gender identity, disability or relative able-bodiedness, and other facets of difference that are important in your community, which might enrich insight and lend new angles of approach?
4. What are some initial ideas you have about projects worth starting? Remember, it is OK to start small and imperfectly (see chapters 3 and 4).
5. Who are some appropriate community partners for your project?
6. What are some foreseeable barriers to your chosen project? What are some initial ideas or strategies for surmounting those obstacles?
7. What might be the role of art or artists in these endeavors? How might creativity infuse your project design?

SUGGESTIONS FOR FURTHER READING

On art, power, and cityscapes

Cartiere, Cameron, and Martin Zebracki. 2016. *The Everyday Practice of Public Art: Art, Space, and Social Inclusion*. New York: Routledge.

Dávila, Arlene. 2004. *Barrio Dreams: Puerto Ricans, Latinos, and the Neoliberal City*. Berkeley: University of California Press.

On expanding ideas of ethnographic methods

Elliott, Denielle, and Dara Culhane. 2017. *A Different Kind of Ethnography: Imaginative Practices and Creative Methodologies*. Toronto: University of Toronto Press.

Kovach, Margaret. 2009. *Indigenous Methodologies: Characteristics, Conversations, and Contexts*. Toronto: University of Toronto Press.

Sanjek, Roger. 2015. *Mutuality: Anthropology's Changing Terms of Engagement*. Philadelphia: University of Pennsylvania Press.

ADDITIONAL RESOURCES

On intersectionality

Crenshaw, Kimberle. 2016. "The Urgency of Intersectionality." TEDWomen. https://www.ted.com/talks/kimberle_crenshaw_the_urgency_of_intersectionality?language=en.

See the film *Tlacuilos* about Central American graffiti artists and transnational crews, produced by Federico Peixoto and Producciones del Gafeto, 2019 (trailer available in the link below, and through his Instagram page, gafetotfv, and his YouTube channel, www.youtube.com/gafetoman:

https://www.youtube.com/watch?v=5Rj9Kktf8ok&feature=youtu.be.

Bibliography

Araya, Mónica. 2016. "A Small Country with Big Ideas to Get Rid of Fossil Fuels." TEDSummit. https://www.ted.com/talks/monica_araya_a _small_country_with_big_ideas_to_get_rid_of_fossil_fuels.

Basso, Keith. 1996. *Wisdom Sits in Places: Landscape and Language among the Western Apache*. Albuquerque: University of New Mexico Press.

Bates, Laura. 2013. "Everyday Sexism." TEDxCoventGardenWomen. https://www.ted.com/talks/laura_bates_everyday_sexism/up -next?language=en.

Berlak, Ann, and Sekani Moyenda. 2001. *Taking It Personally: Racism in the Classroom from Kindergarten to College*. Philadelphia: Temple University Press.

Bonilla, Yarimar, and Jonathan Rosa. 2015. "#Ferguson: Digital Protest, Hashtag Ethnography, and the Racial Politics of Social Media in the United States." *American Ethnologist* 42 (1): 4–17. https://doi.org/10.1111 /amet.12112.

Cairns, James. 2017. *The Myth of the Age of Entitlement: Millennials, Austerity, and Hope*. Toronto: University of Toronto Press.

Cartiere, Cameron, and Martin Zebracki. 2016. *The Everyday Practice of Public Art: Art, Space, and Social Inclusion*. New York: Routledge.

Choudry, Aziz. 2015. *Learning Activism: The Intellectual Life of Contemporary Social Movements*. Toronto: University of Toronto Press.

Crenshaw, Kimberle. 2016. "The Urgency of Intersectionality." TEDWomen. https://www.ted.com/talks/kimberle_crenshaw_the_urgency_of _intersectionality?language=en.

Crowther, Gillian. 2013. *Eating Culture: An Anthropological Guide to Food*. Toronto: University of Toronto Press.

Dávila, Arlene. 2004. *Barrio Dreams: Puerto Ricans, Latinos, and the Neoliberal City*. Berkeley: University of California Press.

Davis, Angela Y. 2016. *Freedom Is a Constant Struggle*. Chicago: Haymarket Books.

Elliott, Denielle, and Dara Culhane. 2017. *A Different Kind of Ethnography: Imaginative Practices and Creative Methodologies*. Toronto: University of Toronto Press.

Engler, Mark, and Paul Engler. 2016. *This Is an Uprising*. New York: Nation Books.

Escobar, Arturo, and Sonia E. Alvarez. 1992. *The Making of Social Movements in Latin America: Identity, Strategy, and Democracy*. Boulder: Westview Press.

Eyerman, Ron, and Andrew Jamison. 1998. *Music and Social Movements: Mobilizing Traditions in the Twentieth Century*. Cambridge: Cambridge University Press.

Faderman, Lillian. 2015. *The Gay Revolution: The Story of the Struggle*. New York: Simon and Schuster Paperbacks.

Fisher, Dana, Erika Svendsen, and James Connolly. 2015. *Urban Environmental Stewardship and Civic Engagement: How Planting Trees Strengthens the Roots of Democracy*. New York: Routledge.

Florida, Richard. 2003. "Cities and the Creative Class." *City & Community* 2 (1): 3–19. https://doi.org/10.1111/1540-6040.00034.

Francis, Nick. 2006. *Black Gold: Wake Up and Smell the Coffee*. Speakit Films.

Gould, Deborah. 2009. *Moving Politics: Emotion and ACT UP's Fight against AIDS*. Chicago: University of Chicago Press.

Haritaworn, Jin, Ghaida Moussa, and Syrus Marcus Ware, with Río Rodríguez. 2018. *Queering Urban Justice: Queer of Colour Formations in Toronto*. Toronto: University of Toronto Press.

Honey, Martha. 2008. *Ecotourism and Sustainable Development: Who Owns Paradise?* Washington, DC: Island Press.

Ingold, Tim, and Jo Lee Vergunst. 2016. *Ways of Walking: Ethnography and Practice on Foot*. New York: Routledge.

Kelley, Bill, Jr., with Rebecca Zamora. 2017. *Talking to Action: Art, Pedagogy, and Activism in the Americas*. Chicago: School of the Art Institute of Chicago.

Kirshner, Ben. 2015. *Youth Activism in an Era of Inequality*. New York: New York University Press.

Kovach, Margaret. 2009. *Indigenous Methodologies: Characteristics, Conversations, and Contexts*. Toronto: University of Toronto Press.

Kwon, Miwon. 2002. *One Place after Another: Site-Specific Art and Locational Identity*. Cambridge, MA: MIT Press.

Landry, Charles. 2008. *The Creative City: A Toolkit for Urban Innovators*. London: Earthscan.

Lang, Tim, and Michael Heasmann. 2015. *Food Wars: The Global Battle for Mouths, Minds and Markets*. London: Routledge.

Lefebvre, Henri. 2003. *The Urban Revolution*. Translated by Roberto Bononno. Minneapolis: University of Minnesota Press.

Leitinger, Ilse A. 1997. *The Costa Rican Women's Movement: A Reader*. Pittsburgh: University of Pittsburgh Press.

Lopez Bunyasi, Tehama, and Candis Watts Smith. 2019. *Stay Woke: A People's Guide to Making All Black Lives Matter*. New York: New York University Press.

Low, Setha. 1999. "Spatializing Culture: The Social Production and Social Construction of Public Space in Costa Rica." In *Theorizing the City*, edited by Setha Low, 111–37. New Brunswick, NJ: Rutgers University Press.

———. 2017. *Spatializing Culture: The Ethnography of Space and Place*. New York: Routledge.

Lydon, Mike, and Anthony Garcia. 2015. *Tactical Urbanism: Short-Term Action for Long-Term Change*. Washington, DC: Island Press.

Marks, Nic. 2015. "The Happy Planet Index." TED Talks. https://www.youtube.com/watch?v=TnA_XxbyKEw&feature.

Massey, Doreen. 2005. *For Space*. London: SAGE.

McLean, Heather E. 2014. "Cracks in the Creative City: The Contradictions of Community Arts Practice." *International Journal of Urban and Regional Research* 38 (6): 2156–73. https://doi.org/10.1111/1468-2427.12168.

Modarres, Mohammad. 2019. "Why You Should Shop at Your Local Farmers Market." TED Residency. https://www.ted.com/talks/mohammad_modarres_why_you_should_shop_at_your_local_farmers_market?language=en.

Montgomery, Charles. 2013. *The Happy City: Transforming Our Lives through Urban Design*. New York: Farrar, Straus and Giroux.

———. 2014. "The Happy City Experiment." TEDxVancouver. https://web.archive.org/web/20191231030300/https://thehappycity.com/project/the-happy-city-experiment/.

Muehlebach, Andrea. 2012. *The Moral Neoliberal: Welfare and Citizenship in Italy*. Chicago: University of Chicago Press.

Munson, Ziad W. 2008. *The Making of Pro-life Activists: How Social Movement Mobilization Works*. Chicago: University of Chicago Press.

Nader, Laura. 1972. "Up the Anthropologist: Perspectives Gained from Studying Up." In *Reinventing Anthropology*, edited by Dell Hymes, 285–311. New York: Pantheon Books.

Nanda, Serena. 2018. *Gender Diversity: Crosscultural Variations*. Long Grove, IL: Waveland Press.

Narayan, Kirin. 2012. *Alive in the Writing: Crafting Ethnography in the Company of Chekhov*. Chicago: University of Chicago Press.

Peixoto, Federico. 2019. *Tlacuilos*. Producciones del Gafeto.

Richen, Yoruba. 2014. "What the Gay Rights Movement Learned from the Civil Rights Movement." TED. https://www.ted.com/talks/yoruba _richen_what_the_gay_rights_movement_learned_from_the_civil_rights _movement?language=en.

Rodríguez Vargas, Marvin. 2016. *En la calle y más allá: una aproximación sociológica al arte graffiti*. San José, Costa Rica: Editorial Arlekín.

Sadik-Khan, Janette. 2016. *Streetfight: Handbook for an Urban Revolution*. New York: Penguin Books.

Sanjek, Roger. 2015. *Mutuality: Anthropology's Changing Terms of Engagement*. Philadelphia: University of Pennsylvania Press.

Schensul, Stephen L., Jean J. Schensul, Merrill Singer, Margaret Weeks, and Marie Brault. 2015. "Participatory Methods and Community-Based Collaborations." In *Handbook of Methods in Cultural Anthropology*, edited by H. Russell Bernard and Clarence C. Gravlee, 185–212. Lanham, MD: Rowman & Littlefield.

Silva, Eduardo G. 2015. "Social Movements, Protest, and Policy." *European Review of Latin American and Caribbean Studies* 100: 27–39. http://doi .org/10.18352/erlacs.10122.

Soja, Edward W. 2010. *Seeking Spatial Justice*. Minneapolis: University of Minnesota Press.

Speck, Jeff. 2012. *Walkable City: How Downtown Can Save America, One Step at a Time*. New York: North Point Press.

Stocker, Karen. 2005. *"I Won't Stay Indian, I'll Keep Studying": Race, Place, and Discrimination in a Costa Rican High School*. Boulder: University Press of Colorado.

———. 2013. *Tourism and Cultural Change in Costa Rica: Pitfalls and Possibilities*. Lanham, MD: Lexington Books.

Tucker, Catherine M. 2011. *Coffee Culture: Local Experiences, Global Connections*. New York: Routledge.

Vargas, Erick. 2009. "ROBINSON: Cuando el Peso Atómico se Difiere." https://web.archive.org/web/20191231023038/https://vimeo.com /21326323.

Žižek, Slavoj. 2018. *The Courage of Hopelessness: Chronicles of a Year of Acting Dangerously*. London: Penguin Random House.

Index

An "n" following a page number indicates a footnote.

Teaching Culture
UTP Ethnographies for the Classroom

Editor: John Barker, University of British Columbia

This series is an essential resource for instructors searching for ethnographic case studies that are contemporary, engaging, provocative, and created specifically with undergraduate students in mind. Written with clarity and personal warmth, books in the series introduce students to the core methods and orienting frameworks of ethnographic research and provide a compelling entry point to some of the most urgent issues faced by people around the globe today.

Recent Books in the Series:

Millennial Movements: Positive Social Change in Urban Costa Rica by Karen Stocker (2020)

From Water to Wine: Becoming Middle Class in Angola by Jess Auerbach (2020)

Deeply Rooted in the Present: Heritage, Memory, and Identity in Brazilian Quilombos by Mary Lorena Kenny (2018)

Long Night at the Vepsian Museum: The Forest Folk of Northern Russia and the Struggle for Cultural Survival by Veronica Davidov (2017)

Truth and Indignation: Canada's Truth and Reconciliation Commission on Indian Residential Schools, second edition, by Ronald Niezen (2017)

Merchants in the City of Art: Work, Identity, and Change in a Florentine Neighborhood by Anne Schiller (2016)

Ancestral Lines: The Maisin of Papua New Guinea and the Fate of the Rainforest, second edition, by John Barker (2016)

Love Stories: Language, Private Love, and Public Romance in Georgia by Paul Manning (2015)

Culturing Bioscience: A Case Study in the Anthropology of Science by Udo Krautwurst (2014)

Fields of Play: An Ethnography of Children's Sports by Noel Dyck (2012)

Made in Madagascar: Sapphires, Ecotourism, and the Global Bazaar by Andrew Walsh (2012)

Red Flags and Lace Coiffes: Identity and Survival in a Breton Village by Charles R. Menzies (2011)

Rites of the Republic: Citizens' Theatre and the Politics of Culture in Southern France by Mark Ingram (2011)

Maya or Mestizo?: Nationalism, Modernity, and Its Discontents by Ronald Loewe (2010)